THE LIONESS IN WINTER

THE
LIONESS
IN WINTER

Writing an Old Woman's Life

ANN BURACK-WEISS

Columbia University Press
New York

Columbia University Press
Publishers Since 1893
New York   Chichester, West Sussex
cup.columbia.edu
Copyright © 2015 Ann Burack-Weiss
All rights reserved

Excerpt of MFK Fisher's "Last House." Copyright © 1995.
Used by permission of the Literary Trust of MFK Fisher c/o InkWell Management.

Library of Congress Cataloging-in-Publication Data

Burack-Weiss, Ann.
The lioness in winter : writing an old woman's life / Ann Burack-Weiss.
pages cm
Includes bibliographical references.
Summary: "Ann Burack-Weiss, a gerontologist with more than forty years of experience,
analyzes and engages with the writings of a dozen well-known authors for insights into old
age. Featured are Maya Angelou, Colette, Simone de Beauvoir, Joan Didion, M.F.K Fisher,
Doris Grumbach, Carolyn Heilburn, Doris Lessing, Florida Scott-Maxwell, May Sarton,
Anne Roiphe, and Alix Kate Shulman, among others, all of whom wrote about essential
issues in old age including physical changes and disability, living alone, reflecting on and
revaluing the past, generativity, public life, and the changing roles of family and friends.
Burack-Weiss frames including an introduction that discusses narrative theory and older
woman" — Provided by publisher.
ISBN 978-0-231-15184-9 (cloth : alk. paper) — ISBN 978-0-231-52533-6 (e-book)
1. Old age in literature. 2. Older women in literature. 3. Aging in literature.
4. Literature—Women authors—History and criticism. 5. Life change events in
literature. 6. Life cycle, Human, in literature. 7. Life change events in old age.
I. Title. II. Title: Writing an old woman's life.
PN56.04B87   2015
809'.93354—dc23
2015008944

Columbia University Press books are printed on permanent and durable acid-free paper.
This book is printed on paper with recycled content.
Printed in the United States of America

c 10 9 8 7 6 5 4 3 2 1

Jacket design: Mary Ann Smith
Jacket images: © Shutterstock

References to websites (URLs) were accurate at the time of writing. Neither the author nor
Columbia University Press is responsible for URLs that may have expired or changed since
the manuscript was prepared.

For Roy
Because he was he
Because I was me

CONTENTS

Preface   ix
Acknowledgments   xix

INTRODUCTION: AGING, I WROTE   1

1. WHO IS THAT OLD WOMAN?   19

2. WHAT SHE THINKS ABOUT SOMETIMES, SOME DAYS,
ABOUT SOME THINGS   33

3. I HAD LOOKED AT MYSELF IN
THE FULL-LENGTH MIRROR   43

4. HOW WE ARE WITH EACH OTHER   57

5. BUT WHO WERE THEY?   71

6. THERE IS A GRACE IN DEATH, THERE IS LIFE   89

7. MY MAP OF A PLACE   101

8. INTERESTED IN BIG THINGS AND HAPPY
IN SMALL WAYS   115

9. JUST SHOW UP   129

10. FIERCE WITH REALITY   141

CONCLUSION: AGING, I WRITE   151

AFTERWORD: BRIGHT AS STARS IN THE HEAVEN
OF MY MIND   157

Annotated Readings   169
References   183

PREFACE

We tell ourselves stories in order to live. . . . We look for the sermon in the suicide, for the social or moral lesson in the murder of five. We interpret what we see, select the most workable of the multiple choices. We live entirely, especially if we are writers, by the imposition of a narrative line upon disparate images, by the "ideas" with which we have learned to freeze the shifting phantasmagoria which is our actual experience.

—JOAN DIDION, *THE WHITE ALBUM*

ONCE upon a time I was a young social worker making home visits to old people in Manhattan; people who had outlived their resources—health, money, family—and were now vulnerable and alone.

After I had made my way up flights of stairs in hallways covered in graffiti or emerged from an elevator that creaked ominously between floors, I would see a bent man or woman propped up in the doorway or an open latch with a distant voice beckoning me to come in and find my way to chair or bed.

Few were gladdened at the first sight of me. "Why did they send you?" "You are much too young!" "What do you know about being old?" I replied as my teachers had instructed me (and I was later to instruct scores of students): "I don't know; but I want to. Please tell me how it is for you."

What emerged was Joan Didion's "phantasmagoria of experience," struggles to get through many of life's daily tasks; a litany of unfiltered troubles from morning to night. I listened long and attentively and asked many questions before answering.

I expected that everyone would warm up when they heard of the array of services available to them: meals-on-wheels, home care, transportation, rehabilitation, money management, and the like. Some accepted the offer of aid; most were wary. They knew they needed help, but the idea of sacrificing even a bit of independence to receive it was hard to accept.

It was then that we moved from their actual experience to Didion's "narrative line"—the stories they told themselves about how they got into this situation and what would happen next. Although most were eager to tell me stories starring their younger selves, there were few Scheherazades. The same one or two stories were told on each visit, beginning and ending in the same place, using virtually the same words, featuring the same cast of characters (the client and others in his earlier world), and depicting an encapsulated event. All bore the patina of oft-told tales.

As different as the particulars, were, each story had an underlying theme. These ran the gamut from pride in who they had been and what they had done to a lifelong sense of defeat.

Once again, I responded as my teachers had instructed me (and I was to instruct scores of students), by delving deeper into the story: I asked them to tell me about what happened before and after the event and to describe the characters and action more fully. In so doing, I hoped to evoke more of their inner lives—dormant thoughts and feelings embedded in the story.

It rarely worked. Details of the experience had faded and only the fragile narrative line remained. The present had no narrative line at all. It was only a disconnected series of events that had to somehow be endured. For many old people, it was as if the story-making capacity faltered along with the capacity for independent functioning; as if the interpretive, sense-making mechanism had worn away along with the cartilage in their aged joints. With no connective tissue or padding to cushion daily experiences, they were left with the mental corollary of the osteoarthritic condition of "bone on bone."

This was not always the case. And I relished the exceptions—current events converted into newly relevant minted stories that connected the individual's past with their present and dared even to reach into a future they would not live to see.

I recall my first visit to an eighty-seven-year-old woman who was both blind and paralyzed, conditions that—to my young mind—seemed impossible enough to bear individually, inconceivable in combination. Asked what she needed help with, she pointed toward her radio. It had broken down and she could no longer listen to the news. The shop she had called offered to pick it up, take it away for repair, and return within the week. "Impossible," she said, "I need food for my mind!"

There were often neighbors or other helpers present on succeeding visits, and I would find her drawing them out on what was going on in their lives. When we were alone, she recounted some of their experiences with pleasure. She was not immune to frustration or fear or lonely moments, but she seemed able to overcome them by continuing a lifelong pattern, connecting her life with that of others.

My final visit to her was in the hospital a week before her death. As it happened, her minister was there. How fortunate I had come just then; how much she had wanted the two of us to meet! We did different things but were really in the same line of work—helping people through hard times. We would surely be great friends. Standing at either side of the bed where she lay hooked up to innumerable tubes, the minister and I exchanged incredulous looks.

It was only later, after I looked back on what I knew of her early life, that I found the connecting thread—the sense of self that she carried into the present. It linked who she used to be with who she now was.

My client had been disabled since childhood. Her adult life had been spent on a college campus. As student and professor she had lived a large portion of her life through the lives of others. She had now outlived family, colleagues, and friends. Though her sense of identity had frayed with mounting disabilities, she had tended it with care, and it saw her through to the end. It was the story she told herself about herself.

It was many years later that I came to connect the difficulty that many former clients had in accepting help with that lack of a sustaining story. The former professor had no trouble accepting needed assistance. It did not diminish her sense of autonomy, the idea she held of herself in any way. She gave and received in equal measure.

She—and others who had held on to the story-making capacity—were not all that different from their peers in respect to life experience. Rather, they seem to have been blessed with a sensibility that looked beyond the transient; a perspective that, while not necessarily religious or spiritual in origin, could be called a search for meaning in their current lives—however diminished in scope. The stories they told preserved the essence of the people they were while adapting them to new circumstances.

It was these stories that returned to me when, in 2008, I undertook writing *The Lioness in Winter*. I had read widely in the life writing of noted women authors grown old. The memoirs, personal essays, journals, and letters of their last years were never wholly about current experiences or recollections of earlier lives. The authors linked the two and continued as integrated selves well into their eighties and nineties. It seemed to me to be the highest elevation of the spirit. Surely there would be inspiration here for myself, for other women who were concerned about their own aging, and for a new generation of gerontologists.

I had just completed *The Caregiver's Tale: Loss and Renewal in Memoirs of Family Life*, in which I summarized and analyzed over one hundred published, book-length memoirs of individuals caring for ill or disabled family members. I did this by juxtaposing a combination of verbatim quotes from the texts with an interpretation based on my own professional experience. It was this method that I expected to replicate in *The Lioness*.

Joan Didion was the first author I considered and could be said to be the inspiration for all that was to follow. She and I were of the same vintage—the years of Joans, Judiths, Barbaras, and Robertas—the girls who were briefly young, busily middle-aged, and now old and alone a decade ahead of the Baby Boomers.

Didion's memoir *The Year of Magical Thinking* in 2005 was about the sudden death of her husband, John Gregory Dunne. It predated my husband's death by five years. *Blue Nights* in 2011 was about regrets and fears of declining powers. It predated my similar concerns by three years.

Nevertheless, I felt myself qualified to challenge some of her assumptions. After all, I had been a gerontologist for over forty years. Surely I had something to say!

I began with a critique of the bleak scenario she portrayed. All the more distressing, I perceived, because the Lisas and Jennifers who came after us, and the Tracys and Stacys who came after them, read Didion for news from a frontier that was comfortably still far away. Recognizing happy images of the "golden" years to be a sham, captivated by her frail persona, besotted by her rhythms, they hailed her writing for its ability to probe the dark places of aging.

I did resonate with the regrets she expressed. I had already experienced more than a few, had replayed the scenes, imagined rewinding the tape, realized that it was too late, too late. I too wakened each day to a self who, no matter how hard she tried to look better than she feels, will never look sixty again. Among the great tragedies of Didion's life—the deaths of husband and only child—she mourned the loss of four-inch heels with cashmere leggings, the gold hoop earrings. Of course. Who but another old lady could understand?

I returned to *The Year of Magical Thinking* in 2010 after the sudden death of my husband, the love of my life for fifty-four years. My Roy, like Didion's John, was taken in a sudden, cruel flash. Less acute but still painful were the names filling our address books; people we thought to call with good news or bad. Until we remembered. Always the dull ache. Sometimes a stab to the gut. *Blue Nights* was even bleaker—the illness and death of Didion's daughter shading into fears for her own future.

And still. And yet. I protested her view of the aging female experience. So hard did I protest that it would not take the insight of Shakespeare or Freud to recognize that I protested too much. When the facts of Didion's life were so familiar, and the style with which she presented them so compelling, it was tempting to succumb to the narrative line she imposed on it: all the good life is behind. Only the fearful present and the dreaded future remain.

"We tell ourselves stories in order to live," she famously observed. But how could the story she made of her later years help her, me, anyone live?

Some criticized Didion for writing from the perspective of a privileged woman. I was not among them. So many of us are privileged by ancestors with the foresight to immigrate to America, sparing us the concentration camp, the Hiroshima blast, war on our doorsteps, rape in our homes, early death for lack of antibiotics or vaccines.

We live on. The largest group of old ladies the world has ever known. We live on to walk the streets in fear of skateboards and to sit in doctors' offices mulling over whose name to place on the "notification in case of emergency" form. The world is filled with privileged women past a certain age who aren't dead yet.

I was well into the first draft of *The Lioness* when, in May 2013, I went to hear Didion speak at the fiftieth anniversary of the *New York Review of Books* at Town Hall in New York. She was one of seven writers on the program—representing the history, breadth, and depth of the publication. A frisson passed through the audience even before she appeared. Stage and lighting crew appeared to be on edge. The dais, at which Bob Silver, the editor in chief, presided over the session and everyone else stood to speak, was removed. A table and chair were run in from stage left. And then— very, very slowly—she appeared: small, frail, expressionless; leaning heavily on the man who guided her to the chair. Without preamble she began to read from a lengthy essay she had written at the height of the uproar sur- rounding the trial of the "Central Park Five," black teenagers convicted of the gang rape and beating of a white woman (and recently exonerated after decades of imprisonment).

The essay was both prescient and a challenge to received opinion. It argued that essential facts to understanding the event were denied or glossed over by those who wrote or spoke of it. Two tropes collided in the cover-up: white women sexually endangered by black men, and vic- tims of sexual assault requiring anonymity lest they be further tainted by public opinion. In both cases "protection" of potential or real victims trumped recognition of unchallenged assumptions and impeded recog- nition of the truth.

Didion read in a monotone, sometimes the pause between words so long that it seemed she would never speak again. Was it her vision? Her voice? Her mind? Neither the applause at the end nor even visible recognition of the crowd seemed to register as she was again, so very slowly, helped to a standing position and walked off the stage.

Watching her slow exit, I had to think that the stigma of old age and the desire to "pass" in a society that honors youth for youth's sake makes cowards of us all. And wonder: what would happen if we began to question assumptions about the inner and public life of old women—how we appear to ourselves and how we present ourselves to the world?

Didion was trying to present an image that hid the truth of the changes going on within her. And ironically, that was the theme of the essay just read—our failure to look an unpleasant reality in the eye and call it by its rightful name.

I couldn't help but think how the night could have gone differently had Didion shown herself as she now was—the same visionary who commanded our breathless attention but different now.

She struggled to read from the original text. It could have been reformatted or enlarged for easier reading. She was unable to walk on her own. She could have used the wheelchair or walker that was probably waiting off-stage. Instead of feeling uncomfortably drawn into a pretense, we would have had to face the facts of life and mortality enacted before our eyes; the very facts that the featured speakers—she foremost among them—devoted their literary lives to examining.

It was not that long ago when Black is Beautiful and Gay Pride were not yet a part of popular discourse, a time when many African Americans and gay men found "passing" as members of the socially dominant group a reasonable alternative to facing the stigma if their true selves were seen. We old women are also stigmatized selves. Just think of how many businesses and products exist to mask the passing of the years on our faces and bodies.

We each draw our own line in the sand when it comes to how we present our aging selves to the world. Shunning pity and troublesome questions, fearful that we will be considered past consideration as fully functioning adults, we stake our claim. Some of us are relieved at no longer having to care. Choosing comfort over style in dress, eschewing cosmetics, accepting the cane, the hearing aid, and other visible signs that we are no longer who we were, we cede the battle. For those of us still willing to invest time and effort in looking our best, choices abound. Ridding ourselves of gray hair is a quick fix. Ridding ourselves of drooping flesh is more expensive, and risky. Freed of widow's weeds and garments that earlier times deemed appropriate for the woman whose days of seduction are long past, we try to select clothing that is flattering to our frames but doesn't look as if we are competing with our daughters and granddaughters. And we hold off on adaptive aids and devices as long as we can.

So I understand Didion's attempt even as I wish it were not so. Even as I try to own changes in my own life, coming, as they did, so fast and thick.

When I began working on *The Lioness* I was seventy. In the eight years of readying it for publication, age had its way with me. I was seventy-four when my husband died. And just as I was assimilating that loss, the severe illnesses and death of close friends, followed by a host of physical problems of my own, arose. Still, I was doing all right until at the age of seventy-eight I fell and sustained pelvic fractures.

Consider a morning three weeks after the fall. With cane and handrail I slowly wend my way down nineteen steps to the kitchen. As I am making coffee, some grinds fall on the floor and I grope my way along the counter to find and dampen a paper towel, bending carefully from the knees, hoping I am not impeding my healing, to scoop them up. Returning upright, I am a bit shaken, and some of the hot water pouring from the kettle into the French press overflows on the counter. And as I grope my way for the dishtowel, careful not to be burned by the scalding water now inching toward the floor, I begin to cry.

Here is Didion's "shifting phantasmagoria." Here is the unassailable truth of five minutes in the life of a disabled old woman. There is nothing I can do to change what happened in reality, but I can change it in my mind.

For help, I turn to the authors quoted in this book. I recall reading passages on Colette's insomnia, May Sarton's constipation, M.F.K. Fisher's tremors. Why are their words still in print, still read, decades after their deaths? Surely the authors' fame has something to do with it. And the style with which they render interesting the mundane details of old age. But the main thing is the story they make of it, the meaning they attribute to it.

The authors do not flinch from their lived experience. Neither do they content themselves with simple description. The experience is placed within the context of all they have been, done, read, and thought—up to and including the present moment. It is assimilated into their emerging identities—the ongoing story of who they are now.

Multiple, cumulative, and interactive, the losses associated with my own aging were predictable in outline if not in particulars. And so, over the years of its creation, *The Lioness in Winter* has taken a more personal turn. The quotes remain, as well as whatever gerontological knowledge and experience I can bring to bear on them. The difference is that I am no longer the omnipotent narrator; I respond to chosen passages with the thoughts and feelings they arouse within me. So the book has evolved into a hybrid of memoir and narrative analysis.

An author tells her story. I answer with mine. And, it is hoped, the reader will chime in. A conversation begins.

ACKNOWLEDGMENTS

THIS book is, itself, an acknowledgment—an homage to the authors cited in its pages and their portrayal of the aging female experience. Most of them live on only in memory, as do the colleagues and friends who shaped my views about social work, about writing, about life. Among the few whose insights influence my every day: Daniel Cohen, Gertrude Elowitz, Rose Goldstein, Carol H. Meyer, Lucy Rosengarten, Frank Rosengarten, Anna (Honey) Zimmer. Their absence makes the presence of those who remain all the dearer.

Thank you to those who—like me—spend untold hours translating thoughts to words: Rita Charon and Maura Spiegel, who gave me the great gift of close reading and reflective writing and supported my fledgling efforts to live up to their examples; Mindy Fullilove, Helena Hansen, and Jack Saul, who helped me see that the story I thought I was writing about others was a story about myself; the Narrative Social Work Group—fifteen strong and growing—who have introduced narrative to a range of practice settings and populations in New York City (long may they spread the word); and my "Lynnies," Lynn Lawrence and Lynne Mijangos, indispensable advisers and supporters through the best and worst of writing days.

At Columbia University Press, thank you to those who shepherded these pages into print: Jennifer Perillo, the ideal reader, whose enthusiasm and perceptive observations spurred me on; Stephen Wesley, who helped me through details large and small with unflagging good nature; and Anita O'Brien, a copy editor with a light, sure touch. Any errors that remain are, of course, my own.

And to the adored quartet who appear glancingly on these pages but are the pillars of my life—Donna Weiss Nelson, Kenneth Weiss, Danielle Nelson, and Jennie Rose Nelson—all the love a heart can hold.

THE LIONESS IN WINTER

INTRODUCTION

Aging, I Wrote

*The frail elder is at risk and in need of social work services when transactions
with the family and environment are maladaptive.*
—BARBARA SILVERSTONE AND ANN BURACK-WEISS,
SOCIAL WORK PRACTICE WITH THE FRAIL ELDERLY AND THEIR FAMILIES

"FRAIL" and "elderly"—with their connotations of disability, decline,
and universality—are not favored in the gerontological lexicon of
today. Younger colleagues prefer "older adult." I revel in referring to myself
as an "old lady." Yet I and my coauthor—both in our forties—reflected the
words and thoughts of 1983. To our credit, the rest of the book did not continue the pontificating tone of its opening. There were even some thoughts
I would repeat today, if not in such stilted form. Still we could not have
known the lived experience until we lived it.

How I loved Angela Lansbury in the television series *Murder, She Wrote*!
As Jessica Fletcher (older woman / successful writer / amateur sleuth), she had
a way of getting to the bottom of things. It was always in the course of an
ordinary day that she was called on to solve the case of a mysterious death.
Putting aside the mundane tasks she was about to perform, she got right
down to it; rearranging the facts until all the pieces fit, converting the situation into a story of cause and effect that made sense. Case closed, she picked
up where she had left off—the business of living day to day in Cabot's Cove.

"Aging, I wrote" aptly describes the ways in which my personal and professional lives have found their way into this book. With an essential difference—unlike Jessica, who figured everything out in an hour, I've been struggling for forty-five years. And though I have taught and written about aging during most of this time and made sense for at least part of it, I cannot close the case and go about my business.

"Aging, I wrote" and went on to tell others what it was all about. I now look back over lecture notes and published works, recall my comments on student papers or process recordings, and wonder how I could have been so sure.

Aging, I wrote . . . is loss. And went on to tick off the ways. They ran so trippingly from the tongue and from the pen! Losses of self (cognitive, sensory, physical functioning). Losses of others (siblings, spouses, often children). Losses of role (worker, spouse, friend). Of course it would not do to leave it at that. So I went on to suggest ways in which professional workers could help their old clients stem the tide of time and went on to quote what others had said or written on the subject, adding a few observations of my own.

I tried to be true to practice experiences with clients and all I had learned from my mentors, to integrate new theoretical insights and empirical data while never devaluing the anomaly. I even included anecdotes that provided insight into the unique human being beneath the label.

Well and good for its time, but its time has passed—at least for me. Like old Mrs. Bates in Jane Austen's *Emma*, who is "almost past everything but tea and quadrille," I am past a lot of things that seemed necessary before. I now suit myself and, rethinking the issue of loss, have more questions than answers.

Longing for a range of perspectives on the experience I am going through, words that open me up to new ways of viewing the life I now live day by day, I turn to the authors quoted in these pages. They did not preach or teach. They simply mined their own lives to come up with a unique view of the aging experience, climbing a mountain of time, pausing on level ground to describe the view.

The texts were selected by an "I" who became a gerontologist when the field was in its infancy and continued as it went through all manner of changes on its way to adulthood. Reflections on the texts were made by an "I" who passed from a young wife and mother to an old widowed grandmother—all the while practicing, teaching, and writing about what it is to be old.

Can one book really affect the course of a life? So many women felt that way that Betty Friedan followed her publication of *The Feminine Mystique* in 1963 with *It Changed My Life* in 1976 to document the societal shift that had taken place. I was one of those women. Even though Friedan described a generation ahead of my own—the post–World War II universe of large homes and families in the suburbs—aspects of what she famously described as "the problem with no name" had seeped into my own later, urban version.

In 1963, with a newborn son and a two-year-old daughter, I was not yet able to do anything *but* read. In retrospect, I was seeking what would later be termed a "Narrative Compass" on which to map out the next part of my life, which was, as yet, uncharted territory (Hearne and Trites 2009).

And the next six years, until my younger child, entered school, I read on, feverishly, about all the choices ahead of me. Novels by men and women, and the developing women's movement, pointed to three possibilities; have an affair, get a job, go back to school. Infidelity? Fun to read about but a fantasy that had no relevance to my life. My husband, Roy, was (as he would remain for the many years until his death) the best. I did not need to sample the rest. A job? I was a typing demon who had even mastered the now archaic skill of Gregg shorthand, but the two years of secretarial work that marked the transition from college to motherhood was not what I wished to return to. School? Teaching and social work were the major choices open to women of the day. I was seeking an expansion of my daily rounds. Teaching struck me as a profession in which life would remain much the same—only with other people's children substituted for my own. Social work was a chance to feed a throbbing curiosity about people and circumstances other than my own. It was an easy choice.

In 1969 my son entered all-day kindergarten and Roy took a picture of him outside the school building—as he had for my daughter two years before. Then he drove downtown and took a picture of me in a miniskirt and fishnet stockings, standing in front of the Columbia University School of Social Work on *my* first day.

It was a heady time for social work education at Columbia University: the "War on Poverty" was on. There was money! Never before (or after) were such funds available for social programs in underserved communities. Never before (or after) were so many graduate school scholarships available for applicants from these communities. The classrooms had never seen so many men, so many older students, so many Black (not yet African American) and Puerto Rican (not yet Hispanic or Latino) students—most of whom brought firsthand knowledge of the clients and situations under discussion. Attention was drawn from the psychosocial problems of individuals to the inequities of society. Heady indeed! All that I had hoped for in expanding my understanding of the world.

New graduates flocked to employment in community-based facilities for youth and families, to drug treatment programs, to mental health clinics newly expanded to serve deinstitutionalized psychiatric patients.

And yet I chose to work with the aged. An esteemed professor questioned my decision. Fellow graduates echoed her view. Unlike those who "had their whole lives ahead of them," the aged were limited by biological circumstance. They were unlikely to change. They were soon to die. There was nothing you could actually *do* with, or for, the old. With so many graduates concentrating on the cutting edge of practice, it seemed that I was coming in at the end of an era. In retrospect, I was a pioneer.

The study of aging was young in 1970. Children of the postwar decade (not yet Baby Boomers) had taken over Low Library at Columbia University, megaphones broadcasting their protests to the throng outside. They were so vigorous. Who could picture them as elderly, bent, depleting the budget of Social Security? Medicare and Medicaid were toddlers. SSI was not yet a twinkle in anyone's eye. No one could imagine what these programs would grow up to be. No one could imagine aging as a field that engaged mind as well as heart and hands, and as a field that would require the advanced skill set expected of today's practitioners.

I wish I could say that deep altruistic motives prompted me; that empathy for the illnesses, disabilities, and indignities suffered by old people fueled my desire to make their last days better. I wish I could say I felt outrage at the lack of services available and saw my task as challenging an inadequate system of care. I even wish I could say that I recognized the Western world was at the very beginning of what later would be described as an "age wave" and decided that getting in on the ground floor would be a shrewd career move. All that came later.

Looking back, I see that my career choice was counterphobic. I became a social worker with the aged because I was afraid for my life. It seemed the very worst fate that could befall you—being old, in pain, facing death, outliving or wearing out the patience of those who once knew and loved you, cared for by strangers. The vicarious experience was to inoculate me against the full impact of the real thing when it came. I was packing a virtual doomsday kit—shoring up resources of information and insight to sustain me when *I* became one of *them*.

I began by making home visits through the length and breadth of Manhattan. From the Lower East Side to Harlem and Washington Heights. From the East River to the Hudson. From rooming houses to cramped single-room occupancies to once grand apartments where loose pieces of plaster hung in wide strips from the ceiling and rats and roaches ran free. My caseload was filled with a group of people particular to that time and place. Most had come to the city in the 1920s and '30s. A few had moved from outlying neighborhoods as teenagers and never looked back. They came because they didn't fit in anywhere else. Homosexual (not yet gay) men and women, dancers, musicians, artists, writers, immigrants from the rural South, Puerto Rico, and other countries who were unanchored from their communities of origin. People with physical characteristics or personal quirks that marked them as different in any crowd. They came to be themselves. And they had made their own, often highly idiosyncratic ways, independently, for decades. Now old, ailing, without family or friends to call on for help, they became my clients. It was a time before funders or regulators were obsessed with "documentation" or fretted about "costs per unit." We were free to visit weekly, sometimes to oversee home care or medical services but mostly "just" to talk.

In 2016 anyone as privileged as I was to meet these men and women would suggest documenting their lives. I picture their pride in showing the world what they had experienced. I imagine the camera slowly canvassing the room, surveying the memorabilia. I imagine the close-ups of their faces and their hands as they explained each piece. That did not happen. They live on only within me.

After a few years I began to work in a large, multilevel, nonprofit nursing home. Although the home was not segregated, it drew its residents from the neighborhood—a rapidly deteriorating section of the Bronx in which primarily Jewish residents had settled in the 1930s and 1940s. What was different from my previous caseload were the stories of my clients' earlier lives; so similar that I could recite the script along with them. Most had emigrated from Eastern Europe as teenagers. Work as cutters and packers in the garment trade, civil service, or small businesses marked the men. The women (who outnumbered the men four to one) had spent a few years as "stitchers" until they married and gave birth to the two children who were now doctors, lawyers, or teachers living in the suburbs.

The more able residents sat in chairs lining the lobby, watching staff pass by—waiting for, wanting, just a word, just a look of recognition. When mealtime was announced, they rose with difficulty, tightly grasping walkers or canes. At night I dreamed of them, outstretched arms, hands like hooks reaching out to me, pulling me close. On weekends I attended dance performances—needing to see bodies in effortless motion, bodies as more than sacks of pain.

The upstairs units—which I thought of as the circles of Dante's Hell—were stratified by level of care need. The worst was the floor of women with dementia: the wails of "Mama" coming from one; another who kept tearing off her clothes. Finding the person within the mask of age was often impossible. Still I tried. In my third year of practice I became a clinical preceptor, supervising students for the three days a week that they spent at the nursing home, trying to teach what I was just learning for myself.

When I had a free moment—not taking care of clients, students, parents in Boston, or husband and children in New York—I continued to read. It was a bountiful time for fiction, written by women close to my own age: Erica Jong's *Fear of Flying*, Alix Kates Shulman's *Memoirs of an Ex-Prom Queen*, Marilyn French's *The Women's Room*, Doris Lessing's *The Golden Notebook*. Along with the poetry of Rich and polemic writing of Friedan and Steinem, the imagined and real lives I read about challenged previous assumptions about how I could be in the world.

The memoir boom—which seems in retrospect to have been always with us—was not to begin in earnest until the 1980s, but biographies and autobiographies were my readings of choice. Jill Ker Conway was to explain why:

> The satisfaction comes from being allowed *inside* the experience of another person who really lived and who tells about experiences which did in fact occur. In this way the lost suspension of disbelief disappears and the reader is able to try on the experience of another, just as one would try on a dress or a suit of clothes, to see what the image in the mirror looks like. We like to try on new identities because our own crave the confirmation of like experience, or the enlargement or transformation which can come from viewing a similar experience from a different perspective.
>
> (1992:66)

Reading fiction and nonfiction, it was not the words but the music, the implicit "here I am and this is what I think," that proved transformative. I discovered that I had ideas of my own and unimagined joy in matching words to thoughts. I became a new persona requiring a new name: Ann Burack-Weiss. It was a copycat move (many women were doing it those days) yet one that yielded immediate and unforeseen consequences.

Folding the Ann Burack of Boston who was her parents' daughter into the Ann Weiss of New York who was her husband's wife and children's mother and coming up with a new identity was bracing. "Finding one's voice" has become a cliché, but indeed there is no other expression for becoming a person in one's own right. The women I read then, many of whom have grown old along with me, gave me that gift.

By 1980 I had found my niche: teaching and writing about clinical social work, slowly, though never fully, leaving direct practice behind. I was to continue for four decades with the field of aging as a central focus.

Until the early 1980s most of the knowledge for practice came from practice itself. There was some research, to be sure; however, the evidence was either anecdotal or based on small studies of elders whose difficulties had brought them to the attention of the health or social service system. So it is no surprise that they were heavily weighted toward a view of aging as a time of unmitigated decline.

There was theory as well—notions about the nature of the aging process that leaned heavily on the idea of life as a series of "stages." Everyone studied Erik Erikson's eight tasks of psychosocial development across the life cycle, the last of which was attaining "Ego Integrity vs. Ego Despair." Classified by later critics as a "grand" theory or "metanarrative," the view was marked by the broad brush with which it painted the aging experience, rendering it as universal across cultures and classes and undifferentiated for women and men, or even for different ages within the spectrum from sixty to one hundred or more.

As a clinician I had learned most from the "practice wisdom" of supervisors who taught me how to observe, listen to, and understand what clients told me. It was clear from the start that the problems of old people could not be categorized as either "concrete" (accessing services such as meals-on-wheels or home care) or "counseling" (adapting to the losses and changes of late life or struggling with issues left over from earlier years). Usually they were a combination of both. Most surprising to my younger self was the discovery that many seemingly helpless clients had psychic strengths with which to meet the challenges of advanced age. Most had lived through poverty and/or immigration to a city far beyond the place of their birth. All had lived through two world wars and the Great Depression. They had coped with traumatic losses and unanticipated changes in the past and would have continued to do so if they had not outlived the financial and human resources necessary for survival. Helping clients recall the strategies that had worked in earlier years and providing them with the support to mobilize and use what remained to them were often all that was needed.

It was how I practiced and what I began teaching. With the exception of *Creative Approaches to Casework with the Aging* (Wasser 1966), the social work literature on aging was slim. To amplify it, the still small but growing cadre of social work professors interested in teaching about the last stages of life adapted the generic social work practice literature of the day. In an effort to put down all that we had learned, a coauthor and I wrote *Social Work Practice with the Frail Elderly and Their Families: The Auxiliary Function Model* (Silverstone & Burack-Weiss 1983). There is much I would change if writing it today; however, the model itself continues to resonate. The metaphor of an auxiliary system that is activated when standard resources fail and shuts off when they return responds to the universal fear that dependence on others (however limited or temporary) is but a step on the slippery slope to complete ceding of one's autonomy.

The book and the model it promoted was adopted as a practice text in several schools of social work, but the times were already changing. The societal implications of the aging of the population had finally dawned on funders and researchers. Less attention was being paid to the psychosocial needs of old people and a greater emphasis was placed on the burden of caring for them.

Funders prodded researchers to find out more about what the population needed help with, who would provide it, and how much it would cost. Rigorously designed and analyzed quantitative studies became the universally accepted method of knowledge building, and it was this received knowledge—perceived as objective and value free—that I was expected to teach.

The obvious fact that age is correlated with health problems, and its corollary, that health problems more often than not result in diminishment of functioning and dependence on others, had previously been acknowledged as but one facet of the aging experience. Now it overshadowed all else. Because research measured care needs, it validated a decline model of aging. And because it sought commonalities rather than differences among older adults, it reified a "one-size-fits-all" approach to meeting their needs. It was not long before research vocabulary and concepts began to permeate practice, which, along with the computerization of client information, was to have long-lasting effects.

Activities of Daily Living (ADL), originally developed as a research scale, soon infiltrated clinical practice. Gathering information on personal ADL (eating, bathing, dressing, toileting) and instrumental ADL (cooking, laundry, bill paying, travel) became the gold standard of client assessment. I recall reading a process recording in which a puzzled ninety-two-year-old woman was asked, "Who helps you with your activities of daily living?" The idea that the client might not view the round of her existence quite that way came as a shock to the student!

Only a decade before, everyone viewed clinical practice with the aged as a process of exploration: individualization was valued. "What is unique about this client?" I would ask students. "Tell me how she looks." "Speak to me in her voice." "If she had a theme song, what would it be?"

Now, back at their field placements, agency supervisors were instructing students on how to best get clients to give the information that would allow them to complete the ADL form: a list of needs in column A to be matched with services in column B. In essence the form asked: what everyday tasks can you do for yourself and what do we have to do for you? The implicit message of the form was not lost on clients or social workers. Clients were seen as a burden; their care needs were all that mattered. Facts were important, not thoughts or feelings. The present—not the past or the future—was all that mattered.

Closely allied was the birth of "case management"—a way of addressing the problems uncovered by an ADL assessment. This often required coordinating services from the "formal system" (social and health care providers) and the "informal system" (family and friends). Because services were expensive and often difficult to access, an employee of a community agency (sometimes but not always a professional social worker) was assigned the title of "case manager" and charged with the responsibility of discerning care needs and providing services in the most cost-effective manner.

By the late 1980s the gerontological literature we were expected to assign to students was in sync with what was going on in the field. Quantitative research was all that garnered respect. Older people speaking of their own experiences might produce phrases to enliven a technical article, but what they had to say was dismissed as anecdotal evidence of no heuristic importance.

The proposal for my doctoral dissertation—open-ended interviews with older adults to discover how they had adapted to vision loss—was denied. Although I went along, producing a quantitative study of the same topic, the process itself confirmed my belief that what interested me most about the aging process was not to be found in statistical spreadsheets.

I recall a panel in Washington, D.C., at which I was asked to present "the consumer's view" of case management as a follow-up to panelists representing the policy and programmatic views. I recognized that I was asked because of my identification as a practitioner but could not resist beginning with the question of why they had not invited a "real" consumer. I wondered aloud if it was because an actual recipient of services would speak at length about her personal situation, "anecdotal" information that would not meet the standards of a professional conference, and went on to give examples of the idiosyncratic ways in which my clients receiving case management services differed from the ones the models were designed for. I was not asked to speak to that group again.

Everything I wrote or taught during that time underscored the necessity of individualizing the older person that was the antithesis of gerontological research and the soul of gerontological practice. Meanwhile, with the gulf between the content I was expected to teach about aging (or, for that matter, other populations where professional writing took a similar turn) and the research literature of approved syllabi and what I felt to be important growing ever wider, I turned to the popular press to supplement the reading list.

Most interesting to me were published, book-length memoirs of ill or disabled individuals and their caregivers. ("Published" because they were widely available and usually well written; "book-length" because they allowed the author space to develop the experience in all its complexity, richness, and personal style.)

My quest for teaching texts soon led to obsessive reading of over a hundred memoirs. The original plan—to write a book that compared the research literature on caregiving with the authors' experiences and to identify the ways in which "real life" and statistical portrayals of it differed—foundered and soon died. I hit an impasse that was to last almost a decade—not of "comparing apples and oranges" but of comparing widely different worldviews proceeding from widely different premises.

How was I to know that what I was reading was not "real life" but the author's version of his or her experience, a "story" or "narrative" that had its own validity but belonged to a totally different domain of analysis?

Strange as it now seems, I was unaware that there was a movement so allied to my own thoughts taking place outside of the realm of health and social services in which I spent my professional life. I was to learn by the simultaneous entry of two new bodies of knowledge in my life: critical gerontology and narrative theory.

Critical gerontology, an umbrella term encompassing a variety of poststructural, postmodern approaches to studying the aging experience, arose in academia in the late 1980s and '90s, alongside and in opposition to the quantitative view that had invaded the professional practice literature. With a shared perspective that all knowledge is metaphorical, historical, and contextual, scholars of many disciplines were united in forging new territory, uncovering the assumptions about older people intrinsic to previously unquestioned ideas.

I doubt if Betty Friedan identified herself with any academic trend, but she held the critical banner high. She was a familiar figure on the Columbia University campus in the 1980s, researching *The Fountain of Age* (1993), the book that was expected to do for the old what *The Feminine Mystique* had done for women—alert the world to the stifled potential of individuals confined to limiting social roles.

Friedan was present at every lecture concerned with aging. First at the microphone during the discussion period, she had neither question nor comment on the topic of the day. Rather, she accused professional experts of promoting a deterministic, deficit view that did not recognize the strengths inherent in old age. Her voice may have been strident and her speech often rambling, but her reputation and passion commanded respect.

The Fountain of Age expanded on Friedan's belief that those who study the old (as those who once studied women) first construct identities for them and then reify these identities through their research questions. De Beauvoir had advanced the belief years before (1973). What was new was an emphasis on the positive—example after example of old people who lived productively and creatively until their last years when they succumbed to what had come to be known as a "good death."

The book garnered positive reviews but nowhere near the interest of *The Feminine Mystique*. I think the flaw was drawing parallels between two dissimilar situations. "The personal is political" rang true for women. Once the finite expectations of who they could be and what they could do were removed, women were to demonstrate that they could excel in areas of life that had previously been unthinkable for them.

The case is different for the old. No matter how many opportunities are open to them or how many second and third careers they try, time is not on their side. Friedan's glossing over the reality of decline and death, her focus on the wonders old people could achieve if society only changed its views and policies, lacked face validity.

The few gerontologists who were at the vanguard of the feminist movement have grappled with the essential dissonance in different ways. All begin with lamenting the absence of interest in aging among the feminist researchers and activists they have worked alongside of for years.

Some continue the lament with a return to a familiar tack of analyzing language as an indicator of societal attitudes. In an introduction to the edited collection *Age Matters: Re-Aligning Feminist Thinking*, Calasanti and Slevin write:

> Feminists often exclude old people both in their choice of research questions and in their theoretical approaches. They often write or say "older" rather than "old" to avoid the negativity of the latter. They may see old age as a social construction and take it as a sign of women's inequality that they

are denigrated as "old" before men are, but we do not often question the stigma affixed to old age. We don't ask why it seems denigrating to label someone as "old." Feminists have analyzed how terms related to girls and women, such as "sissy" and "girly," are used to put men and boys down and reinforce women's inferiority. Yet we have not considered the age relations that use these terms to keep old and young groups in their respective places.

(2006:3)

Others look to mythology for clues as to what opportunities the final stage of life might hold for women. Ray (2004:120) summarizes the feminist literature on the subject. She cites three archetypes—the virgin (creation), the mother (preservation), and the crone (destruction)—that supposedly work in the unconscious life. She goes on to note that in matriarchal culture "crone" meant "queen," a time of coming into one's own authority: "While the virgin's focus is personal, and the mother's focus is interpersonal, the crone's focus is personal, interpersonal, and transpersonal . . . to call forth the crone in ourselves and the culture is to 'usher in another round of consciousness raising,' which challenges negative stereotypes of older women and emphasizes women's development over the entire life course."

Cruikshank (2003) observes that old women are noticeably missing from feminist studies, suggesting several reasons: reluctance of women to identify themselves with their mothers; academic gerontology as a relatively small field; and feminists not wanting to see themselves in their bodies. She concludes that aging is such an untrendy topic that even feminist students and teachers are reluctant to pursue it.

Cruikshank returns to the theme six years later, continuing to lament the lack of interest in aging, and expressing the wish that a time will come when "the 'old' in women's studies will no longer mean fifty and menopause and the great diversity among women over sixty-five and seventy will be acknowledged" (2009:181). She goes on to add: "Narratives are the heart of feminist gerontology and should count as gerontological knowledge. Whether fictional or autobiographical or in the form of oral histories, they provide the nuance, complexity, contradiction, and incongruities of old women's lives that social science research often misses" (197).

Narrative understanding was exactly what I was after when, in 2000, at the age of sixty-four, I—perhaps the oldest teaching assistant in history—read and struggled with new concepts right along with the students in Murray Nossel's Life Histories and Narratives class at the Columbia School of Social Work.

The contrast between the students in that class and the students I had sat beside thirty years before could not have been more apparent. The interest in social action and change had dissipated along with the public enthusiasm and funding for progressive programs. There were fewer scholarships available for students unable to afford the now astronomical tuition. There were fewer men, fewer older students, and, perhaps most significant, feminism had opened other educational and career possibilities for women out to change the world. Many who would previously have chosen social work were now going into law, medicine, or other professions that seemed to promise wider opportunities.

Now—along with an unprecedented number of international students—there was a large cohort of young, middle-class women who—like the students of the 1940s and '50s who had preceded my time in the master's program—were primarily interested in becoming mental health clinicians.

The study of narrative provided gifts for me as well as for them. Although I had prided myself at listening attentively to client stories, readings in literary theory deepened my understanding. I learned to question the relationship between the telling and the told, to look at the structure of a text, to notice what was left unsaid and so much else! The process was the first step in my new journey. It resulted in my teaching the course myself for several years and the 2006 publication of *The Caregiver's Tale: Loss and Renewal in Memoirs of Family Life*.

What to do next? I had retired from classroom teaching and continued with a small clinical practice with older women and began reading and collecting excerpts from the life writing of what I thought of as the Lionesses, noted woman authors who had grown old in print. Or perhaps I should call them *my* Lionesses—women I had been reading since the days before I went back to school, the days when I was seeking examples of what women could be and do in the world. Because my Lionesses were a literate lot, they quoted those who influenced them and my sample snowballed. A few choices came later—triggered by a review here, a recommendation there—but overall the sample remained as it started: a highly idiosyncratic collection that, in the words of Judith Matlack, a dearly remembered English professor, "spoke to my condition." (One discovery of my reading was that Matlack was recalled by May Sarton—one of my cherished Lionesses—as the great love of her life. Such are the unanticipated rewards of narrative research!)

I was working in the home office in which I now sit. My husband, Roy, had a desk at the other side of the room, practicing law on a part-time basis since a heart attack and stroke had left him with a language deficit and physically weakened. At his request, I checked all his written work for tense and spelling. I knew this confrontation with his loss was difficult and tried to change as little as I could. When several errors appeared in one document, I overlooked a few, hoping the reader would see them as typos. "Everyone makes mistakes," I would say when Roy discovered a mistake on his own. I pretended it was no big deal. He pretended to believe me.

We stopped work periodically, as we always had, for a walk, a movie, a restaurant lunch; but as the years passed, we were out for shorter times, closer to home. Everything toned down, muted. But still good. Roy was alive. He was here.

By March 12, 2010, half the "Lioness book" was written. Topical chapters consisted of passages reflecting what many authors had written on the problem—with the barest of my own commentary. It was an interesting project but one with no sense of urgency attached. It was a Friday and I went out to do a home visit at 5:00. I returned at 8:15 to see that Roy had left half of the supper I had left for him on the kitchen counter. Climbing the stairs, I half knew what I would find. Roy's body was lying on the bed, but the man I had loved, who had loved me, for all my adult life was nowhere to be found.

I stopped caring but not living. I stopped writing but not reading. I turned again and again to the Lionesses. I carried their words with me as I walked the streets and sat in the parks of Manhattan. They accompanied me to the greenmarket, sat beside me on the diner stool. They popped out when I was with others. At lunch with a close friend or in a chat with a colleague after a meeting, I found myself speaking of, sometimes quoting, their words. Often I would wonder: What would they think about what I am now going through? What would they advise me to do?

I was in limbo until in 2011 I was asked to teach in the MS Program in Narrative Medicine at Columbia. My role in the program was to help students in the practicum acquire the basic group work skills necessary to running close reading and reflective writing groups. Once again, I learned as I taught. I learned about the selection and analysis of "texts" (poems or paragraphs, art or music) that evoke responses that often surprise the readers. I learned about facilitating discussions of these responses. I learned about designing and responding to "prompts" ("write about a time when") that capture the often inchoate thoughts and feelings engendered by the reading and discussion.

And slowly the cloud over me lifted. I returned to the Lionesses with a new plan, I would pull Colette or Fisher or Sarton from my bookshelf, select a passage I had read, and design myself a prompt. So the book evolved from a collection to a conversation with friends I never met. As Nancy Miller wrote, "We read the lives of others to figure out how to make sense of our own, and in the process we also admit to our wishes for a future" (2002:137).

Taking out the virtual doomsday kit I had begun many decades ago and rifling through its contents, I find that I had packed wrong. Not obviously wrong—as in bringing ski gear to the tropics—but in missing the essential nuance. I had packed sneakers to climb Mount Everest. I had not recognized that the mountain of age was so steep, so rocky, had so many different climates, and required reinforced footwear and heavy equipment. I had not anticipated the many meanings aging could hold for an old woman and what inner resources she needed to survive an avalanche of losses. The Lionesses became my Sherpas, their words my twenty-third psalm.

1

WHO IS THAT
OLD WOMAN?

It is not a surprise to look in the mirrors and think: Who's that old woman?...
And inside this fluidity a permanence, for the person who looks at the old face in
the mirror is the same as the one who shares your earliest memories, when you
were two, perhaps less: that child's core is the same as the old woman's. "Here I
still am: I haven't changed at all."

—DORIS LESSING, "OLD"

EVERY woman past a certain age has had Lessing's experience. It is not a sense of "where did the years go?" (we can all answer that one) but "what can we keep of all that passed between then and now?" What is the balance of "fluidity and permanence" in the identity of an old woman? How can she preserve "the child's core"—as well the essence of who she was through every period of her life since then—as she navigates the rocky terrain of her last years?

"I am downsizing," a friend of seventy-five remarks as she moves from a large house to a small apartment. She adds how freeing it feels to get rid of so many "things" and live with only the essential, the beautiful, the needed. What she doesn't say, but we all understand, is that the downsizing was not a choice made in the thick of her life as a wife, mother, and professional whose house was abuzz with activity, for whom these things were essential. It is a necessity made now, when she is a retired widow, living alone, and too arthritic to manage the stairs of her previous home.

My friend has made what gerontologists would term an "adaptation" to the losses of age. Relieved of previous responsibilities to others, she will now have time and energy to focus on herself. She will devote herself to "wellness," conserving her energy for activities that matter to her now. She will transition into one of the "successful aging" who make professionals feel hopeful about their own old age. Gerontologists have a rosy view. I should know; I was once one of them.

Now that I am on the other side of the desk, I am not so sure. Now that I am old, I ask questions that I never thought of before: How is my friend, how am I, how are other old women now in the first (or second, or third) flush of downsizing to meet the increasing losses of people, places, and things that are now our lot? How are we to face our own declining attractiveness, health, and ability to function day to day? How are we to face our own death that no longer hovers in the distant future but is now too close for comfort?

Lessing writes: "I haven't changed at all." I agree. Inside my old carapace dwells all I once was. That is not the issue. Rather, I ask: How much of that can I keep? What, if anything, will I be able to add? How can I meet my last years with the dignity and grace to which I aspire but that I feel incapable of achieving on my own?

To answer these questions I turned to the life writing of women I admired for help. Most were born many years before me and sent out news from the front before they died. Several are peers—now writing in their seventies and eighties—and a few are Baby Boomers hot on our heels.

These women may have lived in other places, at other times, and led different lives, but age has a tendency to cut one down to size. Removed or having removed themselves from much that had occupied them before, they were reduced to their core. It was this core, who they were now, that I sought to understand and incorporate into my own aging self.

My search for mentors was neither organized nor orderly. I started with authors I had known and read before and branched out from there. My criteria were simple: life writing of women who had something interesting to say, life writing that could open new paths of my own thinking about aging and perhaps help the generation of gerontological practitioners who are working today.

The authors did not lead ordinary lives. Many came from humble beginnings, but extraordinary gifts marked them as special from an early age. Their "specialness" opened educational possibilities while granting them life opportunities closed to many. So it is reasonable to wonder: are they representative of the rest of us—those who lack the words or platform to share what we think and feel about growing old?

Are the authors representative of the legion of old women for whom lifelong deprivations of poverty, racism, and lack of essential life supports trump concerns about the passing of the years? It is unlikely. The freedom to contemplate one's inner life presupposes an existence in which not only basic needs but some of the comforts of life are fulfilled.

A more germane question might be: does the fact that the authors don't represent the experience of all old women matter? I think not. The individual story—whether poetry or prose, fiction or nonfiction—represents only itself. And the truth (or lack thereof) is not found on the page but within the reader.

My present life has little in common with that of the authors. Nor do my early years resemble theirs. There is much in their writing that does not speak to me. As I read of this one's love of cats, that one's deep religious faith, I feel no resonance. Then there comes a phrase or paragraph that takes my breath away. How could she possibly know and express so well what I am going through? Not only that, but her words lead me deeper into myself. Her story opens the door to mine. It is what good writing has always done.

Most of the authors quoted in this book lived large, long, and out loud. Living large was, for many, a matter of traveling freely across boundaries of geography, gender, class, and culture that marked the personal choices of their lives. Multiple places to call home, multiple intimate relationships, working in multiple literary genres as well as trying their hands in other careers.

No one presents herself, nor do I present her, as a model of how to think or feel or behave. Rather, it is the singularity of the vision of old age—the unconventional view on the most conventional of subjects—that commands attention. Reading through her work, I find that Marguerite Duras was sixty-nine, alcoholic, and creatively blocked until a twenty-nine-year-old homosexual man, an admirer of her work, came to call. He stayed on until her death fourteen years later, as an inspiration for a renewed spate of writing as well as to her consideration of him as the great passion of her life. Not many older women could live this life (or even want to), but it does open the door to consideration: what possibilities beyond imagining could lie ahead for any one of us?

Living long, the authors could continue writing well into the upper decades of the life span. (Although a few were as young as fifty, most wrote well into their eighties and a few until their nineties.) Of particular interest in their long writing lives is the fact that many revisited the same aging-related themes. So we read Doris Grumbach lamenting her failing health in her seventies and then read on to see that she is now in her nineties and has turned her interest outside to her peers. Some, like May Sarton, Colette, and M.F.K. Fisher, grow old before our eyes. When we read them in chronological order, we know the future they are facing at the time of their writing and they don't. This gives us pause and a place to remember: as old and limited as we are now, our situations will change, and with them our attitudes.

Living out loud is to notice all that passes between the lived experience and its representation in print. The authors' earlier writing may have spanned many genres; the scope of their concerns may have been wide; but now, in old age, they lean more to the personal. Living out loud, they carry their readers on a trajectory of stops and starts, of gains and losses that parallel their own journey through time. Like many of my contemporaries, they are downsizing to essentials.

The old woman's life, like every life, is the culmination of all that went before. But unlike earlier ages, the opportunities for "reinvention" are limited. While staking out new ground is possible and sometimes necessary (moving to new housing, forming new relationships), it is the quotidian rounds—and the thoughts that accompany them—that form the basis of their writing.

What they have written of their experience comes from well-furnished minds calling on all they have read and experienced until now. Their stories are not "uplifting" or "hopeful" tales written to persuade or instruct. Their stories are tales of their daily lives, of how they have chosen to live out the time left and reflections on what it all means to them.

They write of their decaying bodies, of how they look and feel, of all it takes to make them look and feel better, and of what they do when nothing they try works. They write of being alone in a shrinking world, of what they call on to get themselves through the long days and often longer nights. They write of how remnants of their prior lives stream into the present. They write of their fears and hopes of their last days on earth and what they imagine comes after.

The authors speak to us across time and place as good authors always have—drawing timeless insights from time-bound incidents. They write because they must. And each is sui generis: an observing lens ground from so many elements—life history, genes, personal choices, and the vagaries of chance.

My choice was to cast a wide net to include authors who had written on many subjects over a long period of time, adding richness and variety to the text while adding to the complexity of the task. One such complexity: How to account for the half-century gap of time between the birth dates of the oldest and the youngest? What of the differences in where they lived and the people they spent their lives around?

The passages quoted in later chapters can stand on their own. Yet a knowledge of their place in the context of the author's time adds resonance as we consider "who is that old woman?"

THE TIME OF HER LIFE

Colette was born in France in 1873. Diane Ackerman was born in the United States in 1948. Seventy-five years separate these two women who helped me—a city girl born and bred—find my place in the natural world.

Colette and Ackerman rejoiced in the dawn and taught me to claim it for my own. They got me up. They got me out. How lovely that first light and its promise of the day ahead! What else had I been missing all my life?

Dawn is one of the few things that did not change in the close to four generations that separated these authors. When they came indoors and entered the rhythm of their lives, they inhabited different worlds.

Age—the most powerful "demographic" data—is cited in everything from political research to cereal buying habits. When we say "seventy is the new fifty," we are referring to three dimensions of time, each of which contributes to the substance and sensibility of the authors quoted here.

There is chronological aging, the internally programmed senescence we know too well: the graying of the hair, the sag and wrinkling of the skin, outward indicators of all that slows and sometimes shuts down within us. Although medical advances can now prevent, mask, delay, and treat conditions that befell our foremothers, the old body is still the old body. When we read of the physical ills and increasing dependence experienced by women who were born over a hundred years ago, we nod in recognition. Perhaps our time will come a little later now, but it will come.

Then there is aging looked at from "period" and "cohort" effects— sociological concepts that enlarge our understanding of differences among the writers. "Period effects refer to what is going on in the world while we are alive in it" (Riley 1972).

For our authors, this would include most of the events of the twentieth century: several if not all of the wars, economic growth, depressions and recessions, technological breakthroughs in every aspect of life. From horses and steamships to railroads, automobiles, and airplanes. From stage to movies to DVRs and YouTube. From books to e-readers. From letters to telephones to emails and texts. From outdoor to indoor plumbing.

And yes, from old pieces of cotton cut into rags to be pulled out monthly (washed and hung on an outside line to dry and so notify the neighborhood of the intimate physical details of one's life) to sanitary napkins and tampons.

Period effects are experienced differently depending on the age we are when they occur. This is the cohort effect—the influence of what everyone who is within ten to twenty years of our age is thinking and doing; the news of the world that catches our interest and how it comes to us; what we wear, what we eat, how we spend our days: everything that marks us as members of one generation rather than another.

As I read the authors, I imagine what it was like to be a young, midlife, or old woman at a particular time and place in history, what opportunities and obstacles were a part of their worlds, what role expectations they accepted or rejected. I marvel at the way they continue to speak to us across time and place.

Feminist ideology is present across all cohort groupings. Whether ardently adopted (Marilyn French, Doris Lessing, Alix Kates Shulman), never mentioned (Florida Scott-Maxwell, M.F.K. Fisher), or overtly rejected (Colette and Joan Didion come to mind), feminism is an aura surrounding all life writing of women in the twentieth and early twenty-first centuries. The rights of women—to vote, to own property in the early days, to gender equality in employment and sexual expression in later times—all find their way into the writing.

I have decided to introduce the authors as they introduced themselves to me: through samples of their writing. Formal introductions to the twelve I hold nearest and dearest will be made in a later chapter. Information about the others will appear in the annotated readings list. For now, I hope that arranging them in chronological, period, and cohort time will help readers place them in the context of what was going on in the world as they lived and wrote.

Time divisions are arbitrary; I have chosen four according to dates of birth and the titles commonly assigned to the times: 1862–1909 (fin de siècle); 1910–1929 (Progressive Era); 1930–1943 (Great Depression–World War II); and 1944–1960 (Baby Boomers). Earlier birth dates are overrepresented and younger are underrepresented, reflecting the amount and variety of the writing and my interest in it.

1862–1909 (FIN DE SIÈCLE)

Colette (1873–1954)
Simone de Beauvoir (1908–1986)
M.F.K. Fisher (1908–1992)
Anaïs Nin (1903–1977)
Florida Scott-Maxwell (1883–1979)
Eudora Welty (1909–2001)
Edith Wharton (1862–1937)

Amazing women all! With the exception of Scott-Maxwell, whose single work is known primarily to gerontologists, the others have remained in print for decades and are repeatedly rediscovered as being both ahead of and representative of a time that no one who is old today can remember. Their work has withstood, as the saying goes, "the test of time."

Looking back from the twenty-first century, the world in which our foremothers lived is hard to imagine—from the cumbersome dress required of even the most bohemian of them, through the social mores and boundaries, through World War I, which occurred when they were on the verge of adulthood. The war was so shattering to everyone's sensibilities that it was termed the Great War to distinguish it from wars that proceeded it but also in anticipation that none would follow.

In a reverie of conversations between authors of the same cohort, I imagine Edith Wharton in conversation with Colette. They were both celebrated writers living in Paris in the 1920s and 1930s who might well have met at a literary salon or formal occasion. What would they be talking about? They could be discussing plants and flowers, a shared passion. Yet how differently they thought and wrote about them! I picture Wharton describing her formal, painstakingly maintained garden in Lenox, Massachusetts, and Colette telling of the native blooms she had sighted in city parks and on country roads.

Colette started out as a creature of nature in rural France; Wharton began as a straitlaced member of the upper classes of New York. Internationally acclaimed from the beginning of their careers, they packed several lifetimes in one. Rivers of fiction, essays, and occasional writings flowed from their pens even as they, decade after decade, took on new interests, identities, and roles.

With the notable exception of de Beauvoir, who publicly championed feminist causes, and Colette, who publicly dismissed them, the rights and roles of women did not appear in their writing as an overt concern; rather it was an understood condition of women's lives. What did permeate their work—or at least the work I cite here—was a sensibility that seemed beyond political considerations, a focus (if not always) on the personal, the inner life.

Each, as Lessing suggests, kept the central core of self as life took unexpected turns until their last days. Who but Wharton could write an extensive autobiography without mentioning the one great love of her life? Who but Colette at age forty-seven (and a weight of 180 pounds) could have a love affair with her sixteen-year-old stepson and turn it into *Cheri*, an internationally celebrated novel? Among the remarkable fluidity of their lives, a permanence of their essential nature was evident in the life writing of their last years.

Florida Scott-Maxwell lived during the same years as Wharton and Colette. Her name was hardly known; her published writing, a cupful in the river her two cohorts produced: a slim diary by a woman who had published a few plays in her youth, spent her working years as a Jungian analyst, and now, in her eighties, living alone and not feeling all that well, telling us what she thinks about as she rises each morning, gets through each day, and goes to bed each night. Yet she awakened a generation of young gerontologists—including me—to the complex, varied, and wondrous inner life of an old person.

Everyone remembers Anaïs Nin with the diaries and erotica associated with her life in the Paris of the 1930s. But few know that she continued those diaries through the battle with cancer that ended her life at age seventy-four.

Devoted acolytes were on hand to make sense of the often garbled and elliptic last words of Fisher. So great was the wish to capture her last insights—and those of Sarton and Duras from the next group—that their physical inability to type, hold a pen, even to speak was no obstacle.

1910–1929 (PROGRESSIVE ERA)

Diana Athill (1917–)
Maya Angelou (1928–2014)
Marguerite Duras (1914–1996)
Marilyn French (1929–2009)
Doris Grumbach (1918–)
Carolyn G. Heilbrun (1926–2003)
Madeleine L'Engle (1918–2007)
Gerda Lerner (1920–2013)
Doris Lessing (1919–2013)
Adrienne Rich (1929–2012)
May Sarton (1912–1995)

This cohort was born during or just after World War I and before or at the time of the Great Depression, which—like the Great War—was an unprecedented event that shattered assumptions of life that had gone before. Three of the authors born before 1920 (Diana Athill, Doris Grumbach, and Doris Lessing) continued writing into their nineties, and Maya Angelou, a decade younger, continued previous levels of creativity but with new subjects of consideration.

A defining circumstance in many of this cohort's lives is the institutional racism, sexism, and homophobia against which they had the courage to speak the truth of their lives. Younger cohorts may find it hard to imagine the courage it took to do so. Older cohorts may be inspired to see how that courage now turned to the combating of ageism by their late-life writing that simply says: "I am."

For many of these authors—as well as some in younger cohorts—finding oneself in old age is increasingly finding one's parents. Athill begins the story of her early days with a memorable first line, "I can't believe I have a daughter of seventy," uttered on her mother's hundredth birthday. Angelou is over eighty when she first writes about the mother who turned her over to her grandmother to raise. And although Lessing's *The Golden Notebook* is a classic of feminism—and the oeuvre of her lifetime was deemed worthy of the Nobel Prize—it is in *Alfred and Emily*, written when she was in her eighties, that her inner light glows. In it she reimagines the lives of her parents. What if the Great War that took her mother's true love and crippled her father had never happened? What other lives might they have lived? The ability to see one's parents as individuals apart from oneself comes to many of us, but the ability to empathize with their hurts even as we carry hurts we attribute to them is rare.

Grumbach wrote *Coming into the End Zone* as she approached her seventieth birthday. It is a litany of physical woes and causes of despondency, somewhat relieved by a move from Washington, D.C., to the coast of New England and hopes of a new life there. How could she have known that she would live over twenty years more and turn writing about her old age into three more books and countless articles—something of her own cottage industry—in the meantime?

1930–1943 (GREAT DEPRESSION–WORLD WAR II)

Isabel Allende (1942–)
Mary Catherine Bateson (1939–)
Joan Didion (1934–)
Margaret Drabble (1939–)
Annie Ernaux (1940–)
Vivian Gornick (1935–)
Toni Morrison (1931–)
Joyce Carol Oates (1938–)
Edna O'Brien (1930–)
Mary Oliver (1935–)
Marge Piercy (1936–)
Anne Roiphe (1935–)
Lynne Sharon Schwartz (1939–)
Alix Kates Shulman (1932–)

My cohort of Depression babies are a mixed lot. We are far smaller in number than the Boomers who followed us, and we grew up with far less attention from society at large. "We are getting ready," I heard all through my childhood as the decaying schools and recreational facilities that were good enough for *us* were expanded and improved to prepare for *them*. That feeling of being caught between generations (not quite of what had come before, and uncertain about our role in what was to come next) continued as we came of age.

"The personal is political" was the motto for many of my generation, and it found its way into the work of many of the authors as they began their writing lives. The great social movements of political, civil, and women's rights appear in both their fictional and nonfictional works. With the exception of Joan Didion, who eschews being part of any sort of movement, these women's early works are infused with the excitement of discovery, of being on the vanguard of something monumental that was to change the world. Years passed. Wars continued. Minorities and women continued to make societal advances, but the thrill of being part of something bigger and better than themselves faded. The personal gained ascendancy as illness, disability, and death are no longer about other people, old people out there on the sidelines of social change. They are about them.

Isabel Allende survives the illness and death of a daughter. Alix Kates Shulman cares for a brain-injured husband, while Didion, Anne Roiphe, and Joyce Carol Oates mourn the sudden losses of theirs. Margaret Drabble, Vivian Gornick, and Marge Piercy find insight into how to move ahead by looking behind—returning to earlier years, exhuming past lives and lessons to illuminate their lives today.

The facts that the experiences my peers discuss take place in the context of the world that I live in and that their years run parallel with mine teach me that I need not only look to elders for direction.

1941–1960 (BABY BOOMERS)

Diane Ackerman (1948–)
Alison Bechdel (1960–)
Terry Castle (1953–)

Mary Gordon (1949–)
Kay Redfield Jamison (1946–)
Nancy Mairs (1943–)
Nancy K. Miller (1941–)
Alice Walker (1944–)

The Baby Boomers are here! Are these women truly old enough, is their work lasting enough, to be included in this collection? What do they have to tell me that wasn't said before, perhaps better, by the long line of authors who preceded them? I have mulled that over and come to the conclusion that yes, there is something to learn from those younger than myself. Nancy Mairs's insights on premature impairment illuminate a terrain that most women won't navigate until decades older. Terry Castle and Mary Gordon provide new perspectives on the ways in which relationships with parents persist and change as long as we live. Kay Redfield Jamison adds significantly to the literature on loss of a spouse. Diane Ackerman echoes earlier writers on the enduring power of the natural world to inform and comfort us in our path through the perils of late life.

"Downsizing" is a term that originated in the business world. It speaks of reduction, of a stripping down to basics as the means to the survival of an organism. This concept has infiltrated common parlance about the benefits of cutting back in old age. And while it may work in the physical world (moving to a smaller space with fewer objects to care for makes sense for many), the authors—whatever their time, period, or cohort—prove that it has no relevance in the inner world. Whatever the outer circumstances of our lives, whatever historical time we live in, the core of self is under constant expansion as we change even as we remain the same.

2

WHAT SHE THINKS ABOUT
SOMETIMES, SOME DAYS,
ABOUT SOME THINGS

This book helped us pass the time. . . . The last phase of the work consisted of my
shortening and lightening the texts and toning them down. . . . As a result of
the method we evolved, none of the pieces deals with a topic exhaustively. And
none reflects my general views about a particular subject: I don't have general
views about anything, except social injustice. At most the book represents what
I think sometimes, some days, about some things.

—MARGUERITE DURAS, *PRACTICALITIES*

WHY would Marguerite Duras introduce a book of her transcribed conversations with Jerome Beaujoir with a disingenuous disclaimer? She surely knew that her thoughts—however casually presented—were being recorded and would eventually be published. Far from a "way to pass the time," the effort was a way of satisfying a waiting public's wish to know what the best-selling author of *The Lover* and *Hiroshima, Mon Amour* has to say. And how well she says it! Duras identifies an issue that must be considered in any discussion of life writing: the multiplicity of its forms and their effect on the message to the reader.

She begins with a description of the process of translating spoken words to written text—a process openly acknowledged by May Sarton and M.F.K. Fisher and perhaps used but unmentioned by other authors with disabilities. Does it change what we are reading to know that it was spoken in a public interview or in a private conversation; or that it was spoken into a recording device when the author was alone? And indeed does it matter if the words were first spoken and then written or written directly on a page? Duras does not provide answers, but her description of the method by which her words are reaching us raises questions.

Next, she provides a series of qualifications: "what I think about sometimes, some days, about some things." So the reader is to understand that what follows is not to be taken as a fixed opinion, but neither can it be dismissed as idle chatter. The thoughts expressed were important to Duras at the moment, but that moment—like all our lived moments—is behind her. She ends by a proud declaration that she is not in thrall to any dogma; that, with the exception of "social injustice," she remains open to a change of mind and heart.

Brief, grounded in the personality and style of its author, steeped in her preoccupations, infused with her style, Duras's introduction reflects the essentials of the life-writing experience. Although examples are often referred to generically as "memoir" or "autobiography," these labels are often misleading. What is more, life writing encompasses many other forms: the transcribed interview, dictation, journal, letter, and auto-fiction among them. Quotes from all these appear in this book.

Since the 1960s, feminist scholars have had a lot to say about a woman's "agency" (the ability to speak and act on her own behalf) or the lack thereof. They note that, through the ages, most of the writing about women, in fiction and nonfiction, has been by men, and that the male lens inevitably leads to distortion.

As university departments of women's studies proliferated, there was an imperative need for a corrective. Narratives by women writing their own life experiences were hailed and collected in anthologies.

As the editor of *Written by Herself: Autobiographies of American Women: An Anthology* (1992), Jill Ker Conway introduces the collection. She alerts the reader to the idea that what follows will disabuse the prevailing notion that women have little power to influence the course of their lives. Since, in Western culture, women have been seen as persons without agency, the female narrative with its conception of agency has a powerful appeal (viii).

Section headings of Conway's book illustrate the theme: writing by women who have distinguished themselves in a variety of fields, culled from a variety of sources. Section titles— "My Story Ends in Freedom," "Women Scientists and Physicians," "Arts and Letters," "Pioneers and Reformers"— affirm that these are women who have accomplished something in their lives and that the excerpt we are to read will illustrate how it was done.

I look in vain for an entry that is specifically focused on the aging experience. Turning to a similar collection, *The Norton Book of Women's Lives* edited by Phyllis Rose (1993), I see that the introduction offers an apology and partial explanation.

> As writers try to define who they are, they look to who they have been, how they were formed. The past seems another country, romantic or hellish, equally attractive to explore. So there is much about childhood here, and much about the middle years, as well, but old age is so radically unrepresented in autobiographical writing that any system of organization based on stages of life would be meaningless. For better or worse, we do not apportion our interest democratically throughout the life cycle.
>
> (32)

I am far from satisfied. Many of my most quoted authors—Colette, Fisher, Sarton, Florida Scott-Maxwell—had published compelling life writing well before the editors determined what was worthy of inclusion in their collections. The only possible explanation for their exclusion is that the editors themselves had little interest in what old women had to say.

Then I read Carolyn G. Heilbrun, who, while blaming lack of interest on "biographers," seems to get it right:

> Biographers often find little overtly triumphant in the late years of a subject's life, once she has moved beyond the categories our available narratives have provided for women. Neither rocking on a porch, nor automatically offering her services as cook and housekeeper and child watcher, nor awaiting another chapter in the heterosexual plot, the old woman must be glimpsed through all her disguises which seem to

preclude her right to be called a woman. She may well for the first time be a woman herself.

(1989:131)

The old woman tells her story in many ways—ranging in formality from the autobiography to verbatim transcription from the spoken word. Each of these has its own conventions, its own strengths and limitations.

THE AUTOBIOGRAPHY

The autobiography covers the years from the author's birth (and usually as far back as possible in the family tree) to the time of the writing. It is typically written in chronological sequence, pausing here and there to dwell on a scene or anecdote that sums up a particular time (school days, summers in the country) of life.

The full court autobiography is not much in evidence these days. Slow moving and detailed, it fails to capture shorter attention spans—and very few lives are interesting enough to warrant publication in their entirety. In fact, Doris Lessing and Simone de Beauvoir, authors who wrote classic autobiographies, were iconic international figures at the time and—perhaps in recognition of the limitations of the form and insatiable curiosity of the public—went on to elaborate and add to their life histories in memoirs and essays.

Although the autobiography might have a semblance of objectivity not present in other forms of life writing, it is illusory. Time lingers on some phases of life span, speeds up in others. Anecdotes are selected, described, and inserted in such a way as to illustrate the author's retrospective understanding of their meaning.

THE MEMOIR

The memoir, freed from the requirement for a chronological or orderly presentation, generally centers about one relationship or experience. It is a generous format, allowing the authors to move back and forth in time or to leave their lives for a page or even a chapter to introduce later observations or information.

This book features many memoirs. The form is particularly hospitable to discussion of relationships over time.

The relationship could be with one's parents; Lessing, de Beauvoir, Colette, Alix Kates Shulman, Anne Roiphe, Vivian Gornick, Annie Ernaux, and Mary Gordon are exemplars of this form. The mother or the father or both are interwoven with other materials the author finds relevant to construct an intricate quilt of memory and analysis, feeling and thought.

Memoirs could also be categorized as social history. As we read Lessing, we learn not only of her parents but of the effects of the Great War on many who lived through it. A view of country life in France in the early days of the twentieth century is ours as we read Colette. Gornick and Roiphe were young Jewish girls growing up in New York City at about the same time (what I think of it as "my time" of the 1940s): Gornick in a working-class section of the Bronx, Roiphe on upper-middle-class Park Avenue. Each was unhappy in her own way; some of it related to the particularity of their relationships and some to the social milieu in which it took place.

Memoirs are frequently used to depict a newfound status such as widowhood (Roiphe, Joan Didion, Joyce Carol Oates, Kay Redfield Jamison) with a way of life such as solitude (Sarton, Grumbach). And in notable cases, they can center about the totality of the lived experience of aging, illness or disability (Fisher, Scott-Maxwell, Diana Athill, Nancy Mairs, Colette), or caregiving (Gerda Lerner, Shulman).

THE PERSONAL ESSAY

The personal essay may be a few pages or book length and usually circles about a subject—old age, feminism—in which the "I" who investigates the phenomenon uses her own life experience as a point of departure for making the case for a particular point of view. This book could thus be viewed as an extended personal essay.

Simone de Beauvoir wrote two book-length essays—one on the aging experience, one on the female experience. Both books are an amalgam of mythological, historical, and sociological data all viewed through the lens of the twentieth-century Parisian literary superstar who investigated them.

Other book-length essays center on feminism (Heilbrun, Conway, Nancy Miller), in which the author's wide readings and use of critical literary analytic skills are brought to bear on her own experience as a woman in academia. Or the book-length essay may expound on the experience of place, such as that written by Joan Didion in which the author's identity as a Californian informs her views on the myths of legacy.

Shorter essays include occasional pieces that may appear in journals or magazines. Lessing and Grumbach are both masters of that form.

THE ROMAN À CLEF / AUTO-FICTION

Many of the authors are noted for the fiction that precedes or accompanies their life writing. In the roman à clef, the characters have different names from the author and others described, but their circumstances are directly drawn from the author's life. In auto-fiction, all the characters—including the author—go by their real names and the situations are presented as the author's own, with stated recognition that some fictional devices are used in the telling.

The roman à clef—literally "novel with a key"—is generally written in midlife and fictionalizes an aspect of the writer's personal experience. This is true, to some extent, for all fiction. The defining difference of the roman à clef is that the experience is immediately recognizable to those who read it. Colette's *Cheri* centers on a time in her forties when she had a love affair with the teenage son of her second husband. Lessing's *The Golden Notebook* centers on the political causes for which she is noted.

Auto-fiction is a recent genre. It is exemplified in the writing of Annie Ernaux, whose "I" writes about her early life, abortion, romantic relationships, and caring for her mother, all the while recognizing that compression and sometimes altering of the facts are used in service of telling the story.

THE JOURNAL / DIARY / LETTER

The journal, diary, or letter is a snapshot of one moment in time and, as such, is dramatically different from the autobiography, the memoir, the essay, or auto-fiction. It may be dated by day or month (Sarton, Grumbach) or be simply a collection of passing impressions and thoughts (Scott-Maxwell, Colette, Fisher).

Freed from the requirement of shaping a story of interest or making a compelling argument for a point of view, this genre is a good fit for the author who no longer has the will or ability for a more ambitious work but maintains the need to write.

TRANSCRIPTION AND DICTATION

M.F.K. Fisher sums up the poignancy and gifts the genre provides to authors and readers:

> I am angry because I think it is unfair that at this stage of my life when I should be in real control of the natural talent I have been developing for so many years, which is probably at its peak—yes, it seems unfair that I now find myself too blind to read, or even to type, and I cannot write legibly. And by now my voice has grown too uncertain to be used for dictating.
>
> (1995:263)

When writing the jottings that characterize *Last House*, Fisher was severely disabled. Parkinson's disease and arthritis robbed her of mobility, of the ability to type to write, even to speak. Reading was also difficult, and her words had to be read back to her after transcription. Duras's last work, *C'est Tout* (*No More*), was not so much dictated as choked or gasped out to her young amanuensis in the months before Duras's death.

⸜

Thinking about the many genres that constitute life writing and what links them together, I turn (as I often do) to the clear vision of Vivian Gornick. In *The Situation and the Story: The Art of Personal Narrative* (2001:13) she writes:

> The situation is the outer life: the events, the where, how, and with whom they have spent, now spend their days; families of birth and families of choice, the path from here to there. The story is what they have made of it—the events strung together in an explanatory, narrative way that is meaningful to the author. A story or narrative is an explanation—a linking of disparate events into a coherent meaning; if not exactly cause and effect, a narrative implies an association.

It is this characteristic of "association" that is at the heart of all forms of life writing.

It is not a rundown of activities that consume the author's days that is of interest, but which of these activities she chooses to report and how—the story she chooses to make of it.

We are aware in the reading that each incident, as well as the words that describe it, is set down for a purpose. Sometimes the author lets us in on what that purpose might be. She steps back from the incident itself to draw meaning from it. She reflects on the memories that arise; books she has read, people she has known, thoughts that are generated, all infuse the situation and make it a story. Younger authors, especially those with an academic bent, are more likely to take this route. This is particularly true of Gornick and Didion of my generation and many of the Baby Boomers who came after us.

Other times the activity is simply there on the page and we are free to draw our own meanings, create our own narratives. This is most often the case with older authors, who seem freer to let the reader tie up the loose ends.

This chapter began with a quote from Duras, who is among several writers for whom physical disability dictates the choice of form. If they cannot continue to hold a pen or fingers no longer do their bidding on the keys, they must dictate. If their voices sometimes fail, they must wait in hope of a better day. Transcription of conversations or dictation is not a choice but a necessity. Others find the journal, letter, or diary best suited to their current level of energy and interest, abandoning earlier genres of greater length and formality. Still others—generally those on the green side of seventy—continue with the focused forms of memoir and autobiography. However the old woman's story comes to us, it overcomes the constraints of form to bring us news about ourselves.

As Nancy Miller (2002:15) observes:

If you can't change the history of past events, you can supply a different interpretation, perhaps more interesting, to its outcome thus far. Thanks to other people's memoirs, you can time travel to a former self, though there are no guarantees that you will like what you find.

She elaborates:

You didn't grow up in Ceylon or, closer to home, Texas. You are not now, thank God, dying of breast cancer, or AIDS. But still, you can't help returning to your own life, as if there were some magical meaningful thread leading from the memoir writers to you. The six degrees of separation that mark the distance from your life to another's are really, as it turns out, degrees of connection.

(26)

It is in these degrees of connection that I turn to the authors I call the Lionesses.

3

I HAD LOOKED AT MYSELF IN THE FULL-LENGTH MIRROR

I had looked at myself in the full-length mirror. I took in the scar on my left breast from the three operations for benign cysts that appeared over the years— each time with alarm, false alarm and days of renewed promise in the goodness of life. I saw that my body was soft and the skin from my upper arms hung in small ripples. I saw that my legs, once my pride and joy, had blue veins, at least on the back of my right calf. Like Father William, I was old and sagged where once I had been taut and firm

—ANNE ROIPHE, *EPILOGUE: A MEMOIR*

FOR a long time I had a nude self-portrait of the painter Alice Neel above my desk. When I lifted my eyes from the computer, it was the first thing I saw. She is old, seated in an elegant striped chair. And dignified, from the neck up. White hair in a neat bun, rosy complexion, sharp blue eyes behind horn-rimmed glasses. Below the neck, it's a different story. A humped back, flattened breasts that don't quite reach the navel, a sagging belly, feet awkwardly splayed. Neel holds a rag in her left hand. Grasped in her right hand, in a confident hold, is a paintbrush. She is looking in a mirror and painting herself.

Neel's body—like all aged bodies—holds a history. Various lovers knew it one way, three children knew it another; she alone knew its monthly cycles, its pains and pleasures. Her artistic oeuvre bucked the abstract expressionist trend of her time. Like the Dutch masters, she rendered her vision in a recognizable human form. Unlike the Dutch masters, her subjects—neighbors, friends, and family in the poor, marginalized, mid-twentieth-century New York City communities where she lived—were scorned. She kept on painting. No shows. She kept on painting. No sales. She kept on painting. By the time she was "discovered" and lauded by second-wave feminism in the 1970s, she was old and ill.

A daughter committed suicide. Sons carry emotional scars from a bruising childhood along with appreciation of Neel's singularity of vision and accomplishment. Her body has a lot to answer for. Her body has a lot to say for itself.

That body—a cascade of drooping flesh—was at first all that I took in. Then I spent some time on her right hand and the paintbrush. Getting oneself down on the canvas, like getting oneself down on the page, is work that occupies and sustains until the end of life. Finally, I looked most often at the head. I liked the way she holds her chin up, the matter-of-fact gaze at herself in the mirror that becomes, when the portrait is finished, a gaze at the viewer that says, "It is what it is."

When my twenty-two-year-old granddaughter, an ardent feminist, was seeking a woman artist to write a paper on, I sent her a link to the picture. Thrilled with this celebration of aged flesh, she posted it on her blog. Passing it on, I felt freed to consign Alice to a drawer. Still I look at her from time to time as counterpoint to my reading, what the authors think about their aging bodies, and thinking about my own.

Anne Roiphe wrote the introductory quote to this chapter while in her sixties, illustrating that the "full body scan" of the dermatologist's office can also be performed by oneself in the privacy of one's home. Whether it takes place in front of a mirror or in an internal reverie, deals only with the external appearance or the hidden workings of the elaborate carapace we inhabit from birth to death, confrontation with one's body is a constant in the life writing of old women.

I wonder how many of the authors were introduced to the power of the mirror at an impressionable age through the story of Snow White and the queen. Those first images are as clear in my mind's eye as when I first encountered them over seventy-five years ago. Here is the lovely (young)

Snow White in danger from the evil (old) queen. Here is the queen asking a question of her mirror. She does not want to know who is the neatest or most polite in the land (two qualities I had been lead to believe were essential gateways to love)! She asked who was the fairest. It was jealousy over the beauty of the younger rival that unleashed her fury. Youth = beauty = power. Age = ugly = rage over lost power. Never mind that the old queen was probably all of thirty-five. Never mind that the tale did not spring out of our "youth-oriented" culture but has come to us from age-old myth. Is it not true that our power, our very worth, as women is dependent on the state of our bodies?

It has been ever thus. The following verse, titled "Old Age," is attributed to Anne Bradstreet, who lived from 1612 to 1672.

My memory is short, and braine is dry. My Almond-tree (gray haires) doth flourish now. And back, once straight, begins apace to bow. My grinders now are few, my sight doth faile. My skin is wrinkled and my cheeks are pail. No more rejoice at musikes pleasant noyse.

Bradstreet makes no distinction between the way the body looks and how the body functions. Appearance and health are not disparate entities but parts of the same whole. The bald statement—enhanced by the charm of Old English—makes me reflect on the media messages that surround old women today.

The billion-dollar industry devoted to helping women look younger is matched by an equally vocal industry devoted to helping them feel younger. Cosmetic products are often presented as being "anti-aging" despite the fact that the only anti-aging strategy with a proven success rate is death.

The idea that everyone can "do whatever they want to do" and "be whoever they want to be" is underscored by all the healthful living advice that pours over us from our teens onward. By the time we reach old age, the message is ingrained: proper diet, appropriate exercise, socialization, and a positive attitude are all it takes to live long and well.

So it was that I was at first puzzled about my own changing physiology. High cholesterol! High blood pressure! High blood sugar! How could this be? Of course I remembered how frequently these conditions appeared on the medical charts of my old clients, but that was *them*. This was *me*. I was thin and fit, doing all I was supposed to do—and look what happened!

The truth, of course, is that age trumps all. The body is filled with mysteries and reveals them on its own schedule, regardless of the efforts we might make to forestall their appearance or cope with them once they arrive.

As I began to read, I found that in life writing, as in life, women differ in how much attention they pay to the faces and bodies they present to the world. Writing about one's appearance is most often presented in a humorous vein.

Carolyn Heilbrun in her sixties:

> Several years ago, I was staying in a hotel in London. Leaving my room, I would walk to the elevator down a long hall at the end of which was a full-length mirror. Each day, although I had become marvelously talented at not seeing myself in the mirror, even when applying lipstick, I could not help but view my by now quite stately image as it traversed the distance to the elevator. What was soon obvious was that in the dresses I resembled a walking bolster; in my pants and tunic, I was noticeably less bolsterish.
>
> (1998:128)

M.F.K. Fisher in her eighties:

> My full-length mirror is facing me at about a distance of ten feet from my bed when I get up in the morning. For decades I've slept without any pajamas or a nightie on, except in hotels and stuff. And about a year ago I suddenly realized that I could not face walking toward my self again in the morning because here is this strange, uncouth, ugly, kind of toadlike woman . . . long thin legs, long thin arms, and a shapeless little toadlike torso, and this head at the top with great staring eyes. And I thought, Jesus, why do I have to do this? So I bought some nightgowns.
>
> (1992:91–92)

Doris Lessing at eighty-seven:

Certain events will take place, we know: we have been warned, they never stop going on about it. Teeth, eyes, ears, skin: you'd think there could be no surprises. But I don't remember anyone saying, you are going to shrink. My skirts, comfortable at calf or ankle length one day, are sweeping the ground the next. What has happened? Have they stretched? No, I am four inches shorter, and from thinking of myself as a well-set-up woman I begin to wonder what height qualifies me to be called a dwarf.

(2004:215).

Black humor indeed: produced by the confrontation with the reality of an aged appearance and recognition that—beyond minor adjustments—there is nothing one can do about it.

Humor flees the page in the presence of pain, disability, and above all dread of what will happen next. Doris Grumbach, M.F.K. Fisher, and May Sarton are serial memoirists—describing thoughts and feelings about their bodies in successive pieces of life writing. At seventy, Grumbach (who is to live and write into her late nineties) tells of a body that has already failed in crucial ways:

I have little sense that my body is any longer a good servant that will obey my orders. My ankles have weakened; I am always in fear of slipping, stumbling, and being hurt when I fall. This fear is not groundless, to make a poor pun. Twice I have broken ankles, many times have I sprained or strained them. My arms will no longer lift my thickened body easily out of chairs, out of the bath. My back hurts under the stress of lifting or bending, or sometimes for no reason at all. I stub my toes, jam fingers, feel the irritations of pollen and dust in my eyes, nose, throat. My teeth are loosely rooted in my gums, which have moved back under them. From the pressures of accumulations of fat, my skin has loosened leaving my chin and neck, breasts and buttocks, abdomen and thighs unsightly to me. Everywhere my skin is ornamented with wrinkles, brown spots, roughened places. Cups of flesh have appeared beneath my eyes. My once-firm, reliable body, quick to command and as quick to respond, now moves in slow motion, dry to the touch, weary, lax, unresponsive.

(1991:80)

At seventy-three, she refers back to the earlier book:

La Rochefoucauld: "Death and the sun are not to be looked at steadily." Yet, at seventy that was what I did. I looked at death too steadily and too long. I held it aloft and reviewed it from every angle, like a potter with his pitcher mounted on a rotary stand, like Hamlet with Yorick's skull I inspected its terrors, and saw its threatening effects in my body, in my diminished hearing and unstable gait. Now, having passed that melancholy landmark and looked more steadily at my fears, I take heart from this small victory and no longer stare at death's imminence with so cold an eye . . . and vow to sin no more in that direction. I've been trying to turn what seemed tragic into what it would be nice to think of as comic.

(1993:91)

Later, at seventy-six:

We value most what we have begun to lose: Sight. Hearing. Hair. Teeth. Mobility. Height. Friends. Old age is somewhat like dieting. Every day there is less of us to be observed. It differs from dieting in that we will never gain any of it back; we must settle for what remains and anticipate further losses. I was not being philosophical about this realization, because I was not adjusted to this state of affairs. I saw it as a bald piece of information to be handed down to the confident, the worldly, the strong: in other words, the young.

(1994:9)

Grumbach does not grow more sanguine over time, but she manages to move from self-absorption to a consideration of an experience shared with other old people who are navigating the rocky terrain of aging along with her.

M.F.K. Fisher also considered the themes of physical disability over a number of years. Like Grumbach, her ideas change over time. In her seventies Fisher is a champion of the possibilities of living comfortably with the inevitable physical deterioration of age:

> We must accept and agree with and then attend to with dispassion such things as arthritis, moles that may be cancerous, constipation that may lead to polyps and hernias, all the boring physical symptoms of our ultimate disintegration. Old clocks tick more slowly than they did when young.
>
> (1984:237)

Only three years later her health has drastically deteriorated. Crippled with Parkinson's disease, her voice not even up to dictating, dependent on others, she fights on:

> Of course I shall always think it very unfair that I of all people should find myself unable to read or write or even speak—speak even clearly enough to use cassettes during the evening hours when I feel very alert, almost all of every night. But I refuse to stop. This sounds like pathetic bravado at best. I know it may well be all of that. But I do feel that an answer to some of the physical problems will evolve. It must. It has to and it will, and meanwhile I will try to do something more coherent, and soon, about putting some order into my papers.
>
> (1995:264)

Reading Grumbach and Fisher, I recall what I know of their earlier lives and marvel at how the patterns of thinking and action they established in their earlier work can be seen in their life writing in old age. Grumbach had some success with novels but was best known as an essayist and critic. Her mind seeks comfort in ideas by linking her deteriorating state to the human condition. Fisher virtually created the genre of food writing as we know it today, weaving personal observations and reactions into tales of dining experiences and detailed recipes. Her comfort is found in doing.

Radically changed in body, the authors approach aging as they approached other issues throughout their lives.

Then there is May Sarton, who is prone to use her own experience to edify others. She wrote in many genres, but it is her late-life journals that brought her lasting fame. Embedded in them is her desire to find and pass on lessons drawn from her experience. They reflect the physical struggles of the last decade of her life: cancer, congestive heart failure, irritable bowel syndrome, stroke—each with its implications. After breast surgery she writes:

> I am thinking of making a list of things *not* to say to someone recovering from surgery and in a weak state. One of them is surely "count your blessings"—as though one didn't, and as though to discount tragedy. Another is to emphasize that millions of women have had the same problem like saying to a child who has fallen and torn a knee open, "hundreds of children do this every day." You can't lump people together in a large inchoate mass, for that is to diminish each one's selfhood. No two loves are alike, no two deaths, and no two losses: these are paths we travel alone.
>
> (1980:130)

Colette combines several ways of considering her aging body. In one seamless paragraph, she presents philosophy and action along with a subtle nudge of humor. There is no overt advice in her description of hiding her physical difficulties; however, the proposed technique is ripe for emulation.

> The worst is taking ten steps across the room, walking five yards along the garden, having my night's rest broken by sudden, sharp, jabbing thrusts of pain, reaching out with the quick, impulsive gesture of youth in an attempt to pick up my stick or lift down a book—oh how inveterate is youth, its agility now purely of the mind, and chastised the moment it strains at the leash! As for the stairs, their descent is now a matter of humiliation and guile; for when a stranger passes, do I not stop and standing still, pretend to be putting on a glove or fumbling in my bag! Once the stranger is safely out of the way, I laugh at myself, and my old woman's wiles.
>
> (1963:39)

Most of the authors quoted in these pages did not shy away from using their own sexual experiences in the fiction and nonfiction of their earlier years. The traditional model held out to women born in the late nineteenth century and up to the mid-twentieth century—heterosexual, married, monogamy—was little in evidence. Several love affairs were the norm. Authors who married generally did so more than once. Some self-identified as lesbians; others had sex with both women and men, finding it unnecessary to categorize themselves.

There was no expressed angst about breaking taboos. In her forties Colette seduced the sixteen-year-old son of her second husband and converted the experience into her novel *Cheri*. In her nineties Diana Athill writes that she always preferred sex with black men, who fortunately were attracted by her fair Anglo-Saxon looks.

All the above is by way of introduction to the fact that the authors are often silent when it comes to sexual interest and activity in their old age. We can imagine causes for the omission—diminished capacity, interest, or opportunity for expression coming to mind. However, the reality might be more poignant and many-layered—as we see in those who speak frankly, and to the point.

Athill is eighty-five when she writes:

> The main things I can no longer do are drink alcohol, walk fast or far, enjoy music, and make love. Hideous deprivations, you might think— indeed, if someone had listed them twenty years ago I would have been too appalled to go on reading, so I must quickly add that they are less hideous than they sound.
>
> (2002:3)

She elaborates. Alcohol started to make her sick and she never liked to walk much anyway, and as for sex:

> Some very old women say that it still gives them pleasure, so clearly it varies from person to person. With me its ebbing was the first of the physical indications of old age; my body began slowly to lose responsiveness in my

sixties, long before my mind did. For a while it could be restored by novelty, which allowed me an enjoyable little Indian summer, but when it became a real effort, and then a mockery, it made me sad: being forced to fake something which had been such an important pleasure was far more depressing than doing without it.

(2002:5)

Nancy Mairs was diagnosed with rapidly progressing multiple sclerosis at age twenty-nine. Troubles mount—severe depression, a husband with cancer—yet she manages to raise two children, maintain an enviable career as a teacher and published author, and keep on sending news from a frontier of disability that she crossed all too soon.

At age fifty-three, after reflecting that she is not desirable though still desiring, she writes:

I like intercourse best of all, and the knowledge that I will never experience that again shrouds me in sexual sadness. I have elected, after years of struggle, to remain faithful now to George, but even if I had not, I am aware that men no longer look at me "that way." This might well be so even if I weren't crippled, since a woman in her fifties does not arouse most men to passion, but my wheelchair seals my chastity. Men may look at me with pity, with affection, with amusement, with admiration, but never with lust. To be truthful, I have so internalized the social proscription of libido in my kind that if a man did come on to me, I'd probably distrust him as at least a little peculiar in his erotic tastes.

(1997:52, 53)

Marilyn French received treatment for esophageal cancer in her early sixties. She observes:

It has been rumored that chemotherapy destroys one's sexual drive, and certainly that seems to be the case with me. I had already passed the time of life in which desire is fierce, most compelling (which is the best reason

I know for acting on desire when you feel it: it is not a permanent part of the somatopsychic complex).

(1998:241)

Although authors differ in what aspects of the physical self they address or how they write about it, they share a propensity to reflect at length on their bodily ills. In my early days of practice, many of the professionals involved in care of the aged referred to this commonly occurring phenomenon as "the organ recital." And it did seem that every meeting with an older person—whatever its purpose or whether or not the interviewer had any medical expertise—included listening to a rundown of aches, pains, and symptoms. We listened patiently until the end of the recital when we could pick up on what we had come to discuss. Did we empathize as well as we might have? I think not.

I wonder why we failed to acknowledge all that it took them for our clients to get through the day. Why we didn't ask about the strategies they employed? What we might have said to show that we recognized and supported their efforts.

Now I am the old lady, embarrassed to find herself performing her own organ recital even as she feels a sheer relief in doing so. Each night I turn to the pillbox to ingest my prescribed potions. I still walk but not as far or as fast. I still swim but not as strong or as long. "I still . . . but not as," a general slowing down, is well underway, linked with the knowledge that the downward trend will continue. What will I do then?

The cane I used when recuperating from a fall is now an occupant of my umbrella rack. (It comes in handy when navigating icy city streets.) I do not yet require any permanent "assistive devices." Still, I am taking note of them for future use, much as the pregnant woman anticipates the next stage of her life by closely observing the ways of new mothers. I take special notice of old women with walkers and wheelchairs. They are everywhere I go in New York. On the bus, at the movies, in the parks and restaurants. There are others, I am sure, who look just fine but are harboring all manner of physical woes yet somehow manage to get out and about each day. I have come to see them all as profiles in courage, their bravery as real as that of any soldier on the battlefield.

The full-length mirror trimmed with walnut curlicue that hangs on the wall beside my bed belonged to my grandmother. When I was six or seven, it was my great delight to see myself coming and going as it swung back and forth on its free-standing base. The base had long disappeared before my grandmother died and the mirror came to me. I was in my mid-thirties then. The mirror has now borne witness to more than half of my life. It once reflected Roy and me, through the most intimate moments of our days and nights. Now it is only me.

I do not relish the full body scan—even fully clothed. However, in the black humor vein of some authors, I must admit that my decreasing vision—caused by four separate, interactive eye conditions—can be looked at as an asset: I see the general outline of a younger self (tall, thin, curly hair) without the troubling changes of age.

Even so, I am not above the arts of camouflage. I tell myself that it is not to look younger but to look better; that taking care of one's appearance is a sign of pride in oneself, a healthy self-esteem.

I color my hair but have let facial lines and sags alone. I wear turtlenecks all winter and long sleeves on the hottest of days (vowing that my upper arms will never again see the light of day), but my comfortable footwear is definitely of the senior citizen variety. And so it goes.

I had grown used to being invisible, had all but forgotten what feminists call "the male gaze," until accompanying my visiting granddaughters down New York City streets I became aware of a change in the atmosphere. Men turned around to check them out. There were catcalls from construction sites. And the word "duenna" suddenly popped to mind. That is what I was—the elderly chaperone, glaring and rushing my girls along; they all the while laughing (as those young Spanish maidens must have) at my futile efforts. Do I miss being the recipient of a stranger's sexual interest? Not at all. Do I miss striding along without an ache or pain, in confidence that the physical self that was being contemplated could walk for miles on end without tiring? Yes, indeed.

Looking to the words of the authors, one theme leaps out—acceptance; sometimes with anger, sometimes with humor, sometimes with fear, sometimes with ruses to mislead others, yet never denial to the self. With the acceptance comes resolve—the counteracting of the negative with the positive, the determination to turn the worst of the body's decay to good account.

Physical pain is not sugarcoated. Psychic pain does not go away. What seems to happen is that the authors accept that their physical situation cannot be changed and turn their attention to what can be changed—how they think about it. Their words hold the message of Alice Neel's gaze. It is what it is. Get used to it. And, if you're able—turn it into art.

4
HOW WE ARE WITH EACH OTHER

Poetic imagination or intuition is never merely into itself, free-floating, or self-enclosed. It's radical, meaning root-tangled in the grit of human arrangements and relationships: how we are with each other.

—ADRIENNE RICH, *A HUMAN EYE: ESSAYS ON ART IN SOCIETY*

EVERY gardener knows that not all perennials live up to their names—returning in their season in the same spot with the same radiance. Some are here one year, gone the next. Others lose their vigor before dying out completely. Still others crop up in new spots with a changed hue.

When I think of the people in my life today, I picture just such a garden—a few stalwarts still in bloom, standing out amid the decaying remains of their bedfellows, surrounded by the preternatural brightness of new growth. Rich's metaphors of "grit" and "root-tangle" evoke the complexity and friction, the enduring and evanescent nature of human relationships that bind the authors to one another and to me.

One of the rewards of reading is seeing one's own experience reflected in the perceptions of another. Yet it was not until coming upon writing about the most intimate of bonds—that with a significant other who has grown old along with the author—that I felt more than the comfort of recognition; I feel a knot within me loosen.

While it is true that warm memories of Roy infuse my daily life, it is also true that a deep well of regret often accompanies them. Why did I not get out of bed to look at the late night sky with him? Why did I invariably refuse his invitation to go sailing? More profoundly: why did I not pick up on his many allusions to impending death?

Below these regrets and questions lies a fifty-four-year accumulation of missed communications, quiet anger, long fallow spells. My granddaughters—children of divorce as are most of their friends—point to us as evidence that happy marriages are possible. Their views about us are shared by our son, daughter, intimate friends, and casual acquaintances (I have a drawer full of condolence cards testifying to our marriage as "a model" to others). Still, memories of individual interests and temperaments that pulled us apart even intrude on the last, and in many ways the best, of our years together. Amid the shared pleasures of early morning walks, reading the paper over coffee at a neighborhood café, the museum afternoons, lay a deep silence.

When Roy instructed me on what to do after he was gone, I accepted the direction as if it was his opinion on an everyday matter. When he said, seemingly out of the blue, "I'm ready," I closed off discussion with "I'm not ready" and a change of subject.

How could I be the same person who, for years and years, began each social work practice class by distributing a picture of Simone Weill, below which was written the only question she believed one must ask of another: "What are you going through?"

I turn to three portrayals of intimate relationships in late life: Isabel Allende, Madeleine L'Engle, and Mary Oliver. L'Engle describes the marriage most like mine, a first marriage that has borne children and grandchildren. Allende and Oliver are not married to their partners. Allende has children with her first husband. Oliver is childless and the life partner of a woman. Their words belie dissimilarities of situation and reach over the pages to offer me insight and comfort.

In a memoir that deals with life after her daughter Paula's death, Allende writes of her lover of eighteen years. His children and hers have multiple problems, and they themselves are not well. She describes thoughts that arise while sitting with him in a hot tub:

Willie is no longer the same man who years before had attracted me at first sight. He still radiates strength, and his smile hasn't changed, but he is a man who has suffered; his skin is so white, his head shaved to disguise baldness, his eyes a paler blue. And on my face I carry the marks of past duels and losses. I had shrunk an inch and the body lolling in the water was that of a mature woman who had never been a beauty. But neither of us judged or compared; we didn't even look back to how we'd been in our youth. We reached that stage of perfect invisibility that living together accords. We have slept together for so long that we no longer can see each other. Like two blind people, we touch, smell, sense the other's presence, the way you sense air. . . . With my nose in his neck, I gave thanks for the good fortune of accidentally having found a love that so many years later has not lost its luster. . . . I felt that I was melting into this man with whom I had traveled a long, steep road, tripping, falling, getting up again, through fights and reconciliations, but never betraying each other. The sum of our days, our shared pains and joys, was now our destiny.

(2008:299–301)

"Destiny" is a powerful word suggesting a fate over which we have little or no control. In youth or midlife, the "destiny" of an intimate relationship is finding and sharing a life with the partner of one's dreams. In old age, destiny is the death—often preceded by the decline—of that partner.

Allende's linking of "the sum of our days" with destiny introduces a new perspective. The long, steep road to the end, containing all manner of problems, is seen as a necessary prequel to the end. The caveat "never betraying" is also resonant. I prefer not to limit it to the common interpretation of sexual monogamy but to the wider sense of recognizing and being true to oneself and the other.

Turning to Madeleine L'Engle, I find the idea deepened. L'Engle authored a series of journals under the heading of "The Crosswicks Journals." Crosswicks is the name of the country home she shared with her family for over forty years. Filling its pages are descriptions of harmonious, multigenerational life in a rural setting that reads as a Norman Rockwell painting brought to life: the stranger is welcome, children are born and grow into adulthood, and everyone cooperates in caring for the old. If one word could be applied to these works, it is "rational." So I am startled to see that she has titled one volume in which she discusses the complications of her marriage *The Irrational Season*:

> No long-term marriage is made easily, and there have been times when I've been so angry or so hurt that I thought my love would never recover. . . . I've learned that there will always be a next time, and that I will submerge in darkness in misery, but that I won't stay submerged. And each time something has been learned under the waters, something has been gained; and a new kind of love has grown.
>
> (1977:55)

Reading L'Engle, I newly consider much of my marriage as taking place "under the waters." Roy and I talked constantly about the world around us; yet our deepest conversations were unspoken. The tacit pact of showing our feelings in acts, not words, in gestures that came to symbolize what was going on within, goes back as far as I can remember, through the few icy times when we numbly went through the motions of marriage so well that even the closest observers saw a contented couple to the more frequent times when the shared rounds of our lives drew us ever closer.

In all the long years, we rarely spoke of our feelings for each other. But there is the *ketubah* (Jewish wedding contract) Roy framed to hang over our bed, the tile table he made with our initials embedded in the pattern. Perhaps at the end I never said that the fear of his death took not only my voice but also my breath away. Yet now I think he must have known it in the many small things I did each day to forestall the inevitable.

Mary Oliver is a prize-winning poet who lives with her partner, Molly, on Cape Cod. Her poetry speaks to the self-communing with the natural world. It is only in a rare essay that we glimpse the relationship that sustains her:

> M. and I have plagued each other with our differences for more than forty years. But it is also a tonic. M. will hardly look at a bush. She wants a speedboat; I want to sit down on the sand and look around and get dreamy;

I want to see what spirits are peeking out of the faces of the roses. Years ago M. took flying lessons. In the afternoons I got to stand at the edge of the harbor and watch her stall the small plane over the water. . . . If you are too much like myself, what shall I learn of you, or you of me? I bring home sassafras leaves and M. looks and admires. She tells me how it feels to float in the air above the town and the harbor, and my world is sweetened by her description of those blue miles. The touch of our separate excitements is another of the gifts of our life together.

(2004:11–12)

Once again, I find words to soothe regrets of missed opportunities to share Roy's pleasures. I can now see "separate excitements" as the gifts of a shared life rather than a force pulling it apart. I remember that he was no more interested in poetry than I was in the night sky. I reflect that our solitary interests did not diminish our relationship but enhanced it, making all that we enjoyed together more meaningful.

As I read what the authors have to say about late-life relationships, I recognize with a start that they all deal, more or less, with the giving and receiving of care. A few authors explicitly mention specific activities with which they need help and who provides it. Many more make vague allusions to the people they depend on, and it is only through biographical data that I learned how dependent they were on the services of others to sustain the comfort to portray their inner lives.

As a young student of gerontology, I was introduced to the seesaw analogy of independence and dependence that elders were said to negotiate as their needs for care grew. I pictured a playground much like the one I regularly visited with my children. Swings with young folks pumping high in the sky. A sandbox with those in midlife filling and emptying their pails. A seesaw of old age that could be balanced precariously for a long time, then up-ended without notice.

No one mentions the seesaw now; yet the image returns as I recognize how increasing dependency on others is a powerful (though often unmentioned) premise on which the author's late-life writing on relationship is based.

For the many years that I lectured and wrote about "caregiving," I shared the professional view that those who provided care underestimated the importance of their activity—the unpaid hours of their service and the toll on other aspects of their lives. I also wondered, along with colleagues, why life partners were particularly resistant to identifying themselves as caregivers.

Then came the day when I was seated beside Roy in an outpatient hospital group. The speech therapist began by asking those in the circle to introduce themselves. The first man was living with a more severe form of the expressive and receptive aphasia from which Roy suffered and identified himself as best he could. Next were two women who introduced themselves as "caregivers" of aphasic husbands who were too ill to attend. I was next and, flushed with unexpected emotion, could simply say, "I am Roy's wife."

I could not identify myself as his caregiver in his presence. Could I, as the other women had done, do so in his absence? No, the premise suddenly rang false. I, a supposed expert on caregiving, understood in that moment that familiar and once comfortable labels negated the reciprocity that inhered in our relationship—and in all the intimate relationships I had ever read about or known.

With a new perspective on the topic came the realization that the constructs of "caregiver" and "care recipient" imply that the present is all, and help flows in only one direction. In fact, the care of a life partner—like that of other family and friends—follows a history of shared memories and activities in which now one, now another, performs some service for the other. And if the scale tips a bit when one becomes ill, there is always an effort to restore the balance.

There are an abundance of memoirs written by wives who cared for disabled spouses, most of which speak to the unexpected rewards, as well as the long recognized burdens, of the role. Chief among the rewards is a "time-out" from work responsibilities and a chance to enjoy simple pleasures. Amid pages of frustration at the never-ending needs of her brain-damaged husband, Alix Kates Shulman notes that the simple pleasures of neighborhood strolls with stops for coffee and cake usually reserved for weekends are now daily pleasures.

Diane Ackerman, who cared for her husband following a stroke, touches on another, deeper, satisfaction that paralleled my own experience:

> Caregiving offers many fringe benefits, including the sheer sensory delight of nourishing and grooming, sharing, and playing. There's something uniquely fulfilling about being a lodestar, feeling so deeply needed, and it's fun finding creative ways to gladden a loved one's life.
>
> (2012)

Many wives write of the reciprocity I continued to feel in the relationship—even as Roy's needs grew. Gerda Lerner's book on caring for a husband with cancer states:

> I would not cripple him any more than he was already crippled. As long as he, of his own free will, could do something for me, even just by giving me some time for myself, he was still himself, the man he had always been.
>
> (1985:64)

Reading Shulman and Ackerman, I remember anew the decade in which Roy increasingly depended on me. I was never before—and will never again be—as frightened or as comforted, as wise or as stupid, as impatient or as relaxed, as frustrated or as accepting. I remember how he, too, careered through polarities of response. I remember how he tried to handle everything as he always had, how hard it was to ask for my help, how relieved he was on those occasions when I intuited the need and answered it without his having to ask. All that was in him, all that was in me, was distilled to its essence through those years.

Like Rich, Diana Athill chooses a garden metaphor to characterize the vast underground world of human relationships:

> In a plant there is no apparent similarity between its roots and whatever flower or fruit appears at the top of its stem, but they are both part of the same thing, and it seems to me that obligations which have grown out of love, however little they resemble what they grew out of, are also part of the

same thing. How, if that were not so, could they be so effortlessly binding in spite of being unwelcome?

(2008:127)

It takes some effort to attach the "love" of which Athill speaks to those outside my immediate world; how it may be applied to those for whom I feel nothing more than the interest and concern one extends to colleagues and acquaintances.

Once it is pointed out, I can see how the desire to meet the obligations to care is interwoven with all the other forms of connection we make with one another. What I cannot see, and find no evidence for in the reading, is how one extends the metaphor to the world beyond those with whom one has ongoing relationships. And the difficulty of receiving that care.

If it is not more blessed to give than receive, it surely seems easier. Old people who reject needed care are often described as "fiercely independent." So often is "fierce" used as a modifier that one pictures a wounded animal protecting her turf with all that is available to her. Professional wisdom has it that the marshaling of strength is a fight to retain control, a response to a fear that letting someone in is a step toward totally surrendering oneself to the will of others. Now that I must reach out for help myself, I wonder if there is not also some measure of shame involved. In asking for help we are diminished, admitting to frailty, to being in an essential way "less than" those to whom we turn.

"Whoever you are, I have always depended on the kindness of strangers," a phrase spoken by Blanche DuBois, a faded Southern belle, in the Tennessee Williams play *A Streetcar Named Desire*, is a familiar line to many of us who came of age in mid-twentieth-century America. Long after the character, context, and even the name of the play or movie are forgotten, the phrase lives on. I was young when I first encountered it. Then, I was struck by its irony—spoken to the men summoned to take her away (presumably to a mental hospital) after she has suffered an emotional breakdown. Now I am struck by its desperation, charm incompletely masking fear of an unknown fate at another's hands.

And it is here that the authors provide a challenging perspective. Two memoirs stand out for their depiction of the multiple assaults on self that engender dependence when there is no history of reciprocity, when "the kindness of strangers" is a necessary condition of survival.

The interwoven strands of grief, anger, and appreciation are most evident in those with obvious, visible needs. Nancy Mairs, who is wheelchair-bound with multiple sclerosis, cites ambivalence over accepting the help on which she is so dependent.

> What I need—repetitively, interminably—is help in performing even the most elementary tasks. I can't butter my own bread. Before long I may not even be able to use the toilet by myself. My dependency, in resembling that of a very young child, makes me feel demeaned, diminished, humiliated. This is a horrible situation, one that wracks me with grief and fury for which no socially acceptable outlet exists. What am I going to do if you offer to button my coat, after all—bite your fingers and then freeze to death? Of course not, I'm going to permit you to clothe the naked. . . . I wish I could tell you that I'm doing a terrific job of it, that I'm just the sweetest, humblest little woman you've ever met, but I can't. All I can say is that, in learning to give care whenever I can and receive care whenever I must, I've grown more attentive to the personal dimension of the works of mercy.
>
> (1993:167–68)

Mairs has a religious orientation that allows her to extend the idea of reciprocity to the world at large. There is no such consolation for Marilyn French; rather, she remains in an anger that allows for no reconciliation. Recovering from surgery for esophageal cancer and simultaneous chemotherapy and radiation that has left her in an obviously weakened state, she writes:

> Strangers seem to recognize simply by glancing at me that I am in some way impaired; they often reach out a hand to help me. This is both gratifying and upsetting. It always makes me happy when people act helpful, kind, altruistic; but on the other hand, I dislike being continually reminded of how disabled I appear. When walking, I like to rest my arm on another's arm,

for the support, not of strength, but of steadiness. I know I walk straighter if I walk with someone else. But often the people holding my arm warn me about a step coming up, and I want to snarl (like my grouchy mother in her old age), "I'm dizzy and unstable, not blind!" Sometimes I do.

(1998:124)

Searching for the depiction of care relationships that are neither with long-time intimates nor with strangers, I come upon an interesting insight: many of the authors whose writing concentrates on the inner life are surprisingly elusive when discussing those on whom they depend for daily support. Colette writes:

So, as luck will have it, I am fated to suffer pain, which I reconcile with a gambler's spirit, my ultra-feminine gambler's spirit, my instinct for the game of life, if you prefer it; the Last Cat, towards the end of her life, gave every indication by the movement of a paw, by the smile on her face, that a trailing piece of string was still for her a plaything, food for feline thought and illusion. Those who surround me will never let me want for pieces of string.

(1963:11)

Colette's sly allusion to "those who surround me" is echoed by many others. Although biographical data inform us that the last ill and dependent years of Colette—as those of Marguerite Duras and Anaïs Nin—were shared by much younger men, the specific care requirements of those committed to keeping her safe at home are unmentioned.

Then there are the authors—such as M.F.K. Fisher and May Sarton—who write at length of the pleasures of living on their own. Their journals attest to the comings and goings of others who help with dictation and cleaning, as well as being driven here and there; yet though these others are occasionally named and gratitude given, we never see who does what for whom.

In the last journal before her death, Sarton writes:

An old woman living alone writes poems, cooks up a supper of asparagus on toast with hard boiled eggs, a woman who is often depressed but has learned how minds change and how to handle the down in weeks or months. Still, I am aware that very few solitary women of eighty-two who live alone are as lucky as I am, surrounded by loving kindness.

(1996:345)

"Surrounded by loving kindness"? This is not the "kindness of strangers" that arouses rage in Mairs and French; rage at dependency, which, despite their efforts to contain it, is sometimes unjustifiably released on passersby who try to lend a hand.

It could be argued that Mairs and French are younger and have been visited with disability earlier than expected. These differences—coupled with a changing culture where the expression of women's anger is accepted—could account for the difference. But I think something else is at work here. Something that depersonalizes them as nothing more than care recipients beholden to others for the accomplishment of basic needs, with nothing to offer in return.

Then I wonder about those caregivers most cited in the professional and popular literature—"the sandwich generation" caught between the needs of growing children and aging parents. Here I note the virtual absence of adult children in the life writing of old women. Although many of the authors are childless, several have sons and daughters whom they refer to from time to time; but never as sources of hands-on help. Most often we glimpse their children in depictions of earlier times or as pleasant visitors. As so much of my professional life has involved working with adult children offering hands-on care to aged parents, it is surprising to see how little mention there is of them in life writing of the authors.

Then I reflect on my own reluctance to write of my children. A web of complicated emotions too personal to share and a respect for their privacy inhibit me, the same emotions that will prevail when the time comes that I need help getting through the day. I recall the clichéd phrases I heard so often from clients: "My children have their own lives" and "I don't want to be a burden to my children." These clichés now sum up my thoughts.

How do I escape being a burden? Friends? Neighbors? Paid helpers? It is troubling to contemplate. The authors do not share my reluctance.

They seem to accept help as their due. I wonder if it is a matter of self-confidence; if accepting help at the end of life is but an extension of the homage they have grown to expect over the years. In fact, it seems that those who act as caregivers to the authors at the end of life can best be seen as acolytes.

"Acolyte" is the Christian designation for one who assists in church services: the dictionary definition extends it to "someone who follows and admires a leader." Unspoken but generally recognized is the benefit to the acolyte of affiliation (whatever its terms) with a more notable person. Whether these bonds are cemented in deep affection or opportunism, there are considerable advantages to the individuals who care for famous old people, including access to worlds they could not have penetrated before.

And here, though in a different form, is the very reciprocity that characterizes intimate relationships of long standing. The authors may be receiving considerable care from their acolytes (even those who have recently come on the scene) but take it as their due; after all, they are offering something in return. In their writing, I see total acceptance of the need for help. They are not surrendering their essential personhood in the process. Rather, they are affirming their worth by offering helpers the opportunity to be in their presence.

I wonder if the authors' equanimity in the face of depending on others for essential life supports can be translated to other old women—like myself—who do not have the magnetic appeal of the authors. Most of us cannot offer the benefits of association with a famous person. We lack the confidence in our own worth to see acceptance of help as a necessary step toward retaining power rather than an encroachment on it.

When I wrote *The Caregiver's Tale: Loss and Renewal in Life Memoirs of Family*, I was a different person: younger, healthier, living with a husband who (however weakened himself) was there to support me. Such small things they seemed at the time—accompanying me home from the doctor's office after a debilitating test, heating the soup when I had the flu—so large now that I must manage on my own.

As I now struggle alone with this amazingly heavy weekend bag, that suddenly incomprehensible form, I consider what will happen when I cannot work things out myself: when unknown "others" will enter my door and take over the variety of chores necessary to get me through the day.

Turning the authors' experience to my own use and that of others who are old or work with the aged, I think again of reciprocity: what do I, what does anyone have to offer the younger, more able people who appear to help us as we reach the end?

I recently had a preview at the drugstore. The assemblage of the prescribed blood pressure monitor was beyond my visual or manual capacities. How was I to install the batteries? Why couldn't I get it wound up the way the way they did in the doctor's office? I asked the young man behind the counter if he could help me, and, if so, when would be a convenient time. He suggested returning at another hour. When I did, I found him not only ready but pumped up with pride as he exhibited his handiwork. Here it was: fully charged, just the right width to slip onto my skinny arm. My shame at needing help at such a simple task evaporated when I saw how good he felt about what he had done.

Could my experience at the drugstore be converted to help within my home when that day comes? I imagine the authors and their helpers in conversation—not about the tasks performed or the need for them but about the world of today and how the elder's experience may help the younger through it. Theirs might be a rarified discussion, but mine needn't be. Any topic will do. Every old person has something of herself to give: a recipe, a way of stacking laundry, family experiences that might echo or inform the helper's own.

In years of social work practice, I have seen such reciprocal relationships arise spontaneously and noted their benefits but never thought deeply about them. Now I see that although the old woman may seem to have nothing to offer in return for the help she receives, she may well be—like Lear's Cordelia—"herself a dowry."

Those of us who came of age before the digital revolution have well-worn address/phone books that tell a story. Names once woven into the fabric of our days, long disappeared to places unknown. Names whose decline we can trace through moves to ever-smaller living quarters. Names we will never again write or call, not needing to receive a "No forwarding address" or "Discontinued service" notification to inform us of the final move.

Among the many names that have passed through my book (whole pages that I could draw a line through if I wished), there are a few new names, people lately met and not as deeply known but welcome new growth in the spent garden.

Rich's garden metaphors of "grit" and "root-entangled" instruct as well as describe the late-life landscape of human relationships. Old blooms die while their underground roots nurture new seedlings in mysterious ways.

5

BUT WHO WERE THEY?

*But who were they? Though I've squinted through the keyhole at their past,
read through their private letters and manuscripts, I still can't say. Not only
because my self-regard kept me ignorant of their lives but because like every
parent they presented personae designed to protect now their children, now
themselves.... How can one peer through the windows of one's parents' lives
without encountering one's own opaque reflection.*

—ALIX KATES SHULMAN, *A GOOD ENOUGH DAUGHTER*

WHEN we are young we don't give a thought to who *they* were; defining ourselves, often in opposition to *them*, is what we're after. Until we grow old, older than they are in our memories, perhaps older than they were when they died. As the passage of time brings us to a consideration of our own ends, many of us think more and more of our parents. The mystery of who they were and what of them lives on in us grows deeper, the need to unravel it more essential.

My parents, now dead for over thirty years, live on within me. When I least expect it, a childhood memory or emotion rises up and all but engulfs me with its power. So many memories! The meanings so contradictory! I sift through them in a state of frustration—trying to make some sense of it. I turn again to my authors. What did they do with it all?

Past masters at the construction of stories in a variety of genres, the authors gather the old pictures, revisit the family legends, consider this clock or that vase—objects that came all the way from there and then to here and now. They reimagine scenes and dialogue, speculating on motivations, wondering about alternative endings. I follow their lead.

I have the picture right here. She was Polly. He was Bob. They must have been in their forties—seated at a table, his arm around her shoulder, half smiles that look a bit startled. It is one of those photos taken by a roving photographer at an event. I see the back of the person beside her, half faces at another table behind. I remember the dress and her pleasure at having found it—navy with a pearl-encrusted Peter Pan collar. She still had the distinctive widow's peak; it would be years until her hair (every single one—lashes, eyebrows, pubis) was lost in a drug detoxification effort, never to return. Psychiatric hospitalizations, electroshock treatments, and outpatient treatments were behind and ahead of her, but for this brief moment she looks okay. In fact, she looks as if she might be having a good time. Yet he, who usually has a good time, looks stiff. What has interfered with his habitual joy in a social occasion? Is it, perhaps, that he is afraid of what she may say or do next?

I have looked at this picture many times through the years. It has an old frame and wire. Someone thought it important enough to go to the trouble of taking it into downtown Boston to have this done and bringing it back to the apartment to hang on the wall. Who did this? Where was it hung? And why? I don't remember any pictures on the walls during those years. Now my adult self reads all sorts of things into it, piecing together a puzzle that seems essential to get right.

In an acclaimed memoir of her long apprenticeship as a writer, Eudora Welty writes:

> It seems to me, writing of my parents now in my seventies, that I see continuities in their lives that weren't visible to me when they were living. Even at the times that have left me my most vivid memories of them, there were connections between them that escaped me. Could it be because I can better see their lives—or any lives I know—today because I'm a fiction writer? See

them not as fiction, certainly—see them, perhaps as even greater mysteries than I knew. Writing fiction has developed in me an abiding respect for the unknown in a human lifetime and a sense where to look for the threads, how to follow, how to connect, find in the thick of the tangle what clear line persists. The strands are all there: to the memory nothing is ever lost.

(1983:98)

It came naturally to me to write of Polly and Bob. Only later did I realize that many of the authors write about their parents in the third person, viewing their mothers and fathers as if from afar. I now wonder if I was merely copying a familiar form or if I was telling myself how close I want to get. Perhaps both are true. When it comes to making sense of our parents' lives, confusion and ambiguity abound.

I did not place the photograph of Polly and Bob in a historical or geographical context, but it is surely there: the "dressing up" to go to a party, the photographer who goes from table to table taking names and addresses, later developing the prints and sending them out, hoping that he will sell enough to make it worth his while, speak to a time (the early 1950s) and world (suburban United States) that are inseparable from their personal lives.

In a memoir centered on powerful people who have influenced her life and work, May Sarton introduces her parents through an inscription she finds in a book of Walt Whitman that was a gift from her mother to her father. She then uses the third person to place her parents and self in the context of history:

> "George from Mabel, August 31, 1910." She adds. "And as Mabel Elwes chose this present for the man she was to marry, she an English girl, he a Belgian young man—a book celebrating the New World—she was being carried forward without knowing it into a pattern that is now visible. They were to become Americans, these two, and the foreign poet a compatriot. They were to have one child, who would find the book and the inscription after their deaths, and see in a flash the whole cycle of their lives, its apparent violent dislocations, its inner harmony.

(I KNEW A PHOENIX, 98)

Adrienne Rich also looks to the written documents a parent has left behind; to a time and place long gone—a time when women's place in the world was clearly defined. It takes only a one-line entry from her mother's notebook to get her going on a bitter riff where she acknowledges "my mother" and "my parents"—but with only one exception refers to herself as "the child" or "she." In doing so she gains distance not only from her parents but from her childhood self—the better to portray the remembered pain.

> *This is the child we needed and deserved*, my mother writes in a notebook when I'm three. My parents require a perfectly developing child, evidence of their intelligence and culture. I'm kept from school, taught at home till the age of nine. My mother once an aspiring pianist and composer who earned her living as a piano teacher need not—must not—work for money after marriage. Within this bubble of class privilege, the child can be educated at home, taught to play Mozart on the piano at four years old. She develops facial tics, eczema in the creases of her elbows and knees, hay fever. She is prohibited confusion; her lessons and accomplishments must follow a clear trajectory. For her parents she is living proof. A Black woman cleans the apartment, cooks, takes care of the child when the child isn't being "educated."
>
> (2003:184)

Reading this and remembering that Rich survived to challenge gender roles in powerful poems and essays that influenced a generation of feminists. I note that her writing carries the confidence and polemical quality of her mother's notebook entry. The daughter who broke the bounds of what "must not" be done nevertheless retains her mother's voice!

The first person/third person depiction—in which the daughter remains "I," viewing her parents from a distance and in a historical perspective, reaches an apotheosis with Doris Lessing. At age eighty-eight, after winning the Nobel Prize in Literature for decades of distinguished literary work, Lessing published *Alfred and Emily*. The frontispiece consists of formal photographs of her parents when young. In the preface she notes:

That war, the Great War, the war that would end all war, squatted over my childhood. The trenches were as present to me as anything I actually saw around me. And here I still am, trying to get out from under that monstrous legacy, trying to get free. . . . If I could meet Alfred Tayler and Emily McVeigh now, as I have written them, as they might have been had the Great War not happened, I hope they would appreciate the lives I have given them.

(2008:VIII)

The book is divided into two parts: part 1 is *Alfred and Emily: A Novella.* In it, Lessing imagines her parents lives if World War I had never happened. Alfred is a healthy, happy farmer. Emily marries a doctor who dies young, leaving her a rich, philanthropic widow. Alfred dies "a very old man." Emily dies at the age she did (seventy-three) but after a heroic encounter with boys tormenting a dog. "Hundreds of people came to her funeral" (138).

Part 2 is *Alfred and Emily; Two Lives.* In it, Lessing tells the true story. Alfred is seriously injured in the war, Emily, his nurse, becomes his wife and downtrodden caregiver, broken down with the disappointments of life.

At the end of part 2, Lessing observes:

One may write a life in five volumes, or in a sentence. How about this? Alfred Tayler, a vigorous and healthy man, was wounded badly in the First World War, tried to live as if he were not incapacitated, illnesses defeated him, and at the end of a shortened life he was begging, "You put a sick old dog out of his misery, why not me?"

(152)

In the fictional account there is a colon before *A Novella.* Fiction is whatever the author imagines—her indisputable truth. In the memoir there is a semicolon before *Two Lives.* A semicolon indicates continuance without closure—so much that is never known, that never can be known. And here is Lessing, after all her years, all her public acclaim, "still struggling to be free."

We were always referred to as a unit: "Polly, Bob, and Ann," Bob and Ann, Polly and Ann. Each relationship was a fixed star in my early universe. And continues to shed clouded light.

The story of how Polly and Bob got together: She was the beautiful girl from the "best family" with something wrong with her that no one could quite put their finger on. He was the poor boy who was ready to run after the first sign of craziness appeared—brought back by a mother who couldn't let an opportunity for one of her children to lift his station pass by.

The story of how I came to be: Polly developed eczema on their honeymoon and returned to live with her parents for five years after. *Five* years? Well the rash did cover her whole body, itched interminably, and steroids had yet to be developed. She took up knitting. What with the hourly baths and compresses, there was nothing much else she could do. Bob's mother—hopeful until now—saw it as a bad sign. "She knits and knits. She will *never* give you a child." (When and where did I hear these words that initiated the effort to conceive me? I can't imagine. They are so clear, so loud, that it is as if they were spoken to me.)

The jig was up. Polly would live as a wife to Bob or the marriage was over. A shanda (a shame) on both families at a time when divorce was rare. So they got together and, within a year, I came to be. Was it the only time they had sex? I have no siblings and saw no indication of an intimate life, but who knows? Who ever knows?

They were to stay married until her death—in her sleep, in the psychiatric unit of a general hospital. He was to die in his sleep at home three months later. And I was left to come from New York every few years to stand by their stones in the cemetery in West Roxbury. Robert Burack, Beloved Husband and Father; Pauline Levinson Burack, Beloved Wife and Mother.

As I continue to write my own story, I recognize that viewing my parents as Polly and Bob frees me to write of them in a different way—although I cannot yet identify exactly where this will take me. I read on.

Annie Ernaux is a well-regarded exponent of the genre of auto-fiction in which all characters (including herself) bear their real names and the lives portrayed are their own. The titles of two of her works, *A Woman's Story*, based on her mother, and *A Man's Place*, based on her father, illustrate her desire to elevate their individual lives to a generalized portrait. A paragraph early in *A Woman's Story* reflects this purpose, her awareness of its incomplete realization, and the complexity of the task.

> I would also like to capture the real woman, the one who existed independently from me, born on the outskirts of a small Normandy town, and who died in the geriatric ward of a hospital in the suburbs of Paris. The more objective aspect of my writing will probably involve a cross between family history and sociology, reality and fiction. This book can be seen as a literary venture as its purpose is to find out the truth about my mother, a truth that can be conveyed only by words. (Neither photographs, nor my own memories, nor even the reminiscences of my family can bring me this truth.)
>
> (1988:12)

Ernaux—like Sarton, Lessing, and Rich—anchors her parents in their time and place in history. There is affection as well as condescension in Ernaux's portrayal of her parents' lives, as if they are interesting "characters" with no relation to her. Of her father's late life when the small general store in their rural village was made obsolete by the first supermarket, she writes:

> He started thinking about selling the business. They could move into the adjoining house, which they must have bought at the same time as the shop: a two-roomed flat with a kitchen and cellar. He would salvage some tins and a few good bottles of wine. He would keep hens for fresh eggs. They could come and see us in the Haute-Savoie. He already had the satisfaction of being on the health service at the age of sixty-five. When he got back from the chemist, he loved to settle at the table and arrange the stickers on his reimbursement sheet. He enjoyed life more and more.
>
> (1992:79)

Central to the story of both her parents is Ernaux's own growing distance from their reality. It is here she stops speaking of A Woman and A Man and places herself front and center in the story of their lives.

> Away from home I had stripped my parents of their speech and mannerisms, turning them into magnificent people. Now I was hearing their real voices again—loud and booming—and their broad Norman pronunciation, saying "a" in place of "elle." I realized they had always been like this, without the "decorum" and the language which I now considered to be normal. I felt torn between two identities.
>
> (78)

She ends *A Woman's Story*:

> A few weeks ago, one of my aunts told me that when my mother and father started going out together, they would arrange to meet in the lavatories at the rope factory. Now that my mother is dead, I wouldn't want to learn anything about her that I hadn't known when she was alive.
>
> (89)

She ends *A Man's Place*:

> Now I have finished taking possession of the legacy with which I had to part when I entered the educated, bourgeois world.
>
> (87)

Ernaux might not have known it at the time, but she is not yet "finished." Her mother lives on to develop Alzheimer's disease and spend the years before her death in a nursing home, years that she documents in a dated diary, facing for the first time that she did not part from the legacy, that it lives on within her: "I notice that I have inherited her brusque, violent temper, as well as a tendency to seize things and throw them down with fury. A. pointed this out to me" (1999:66).

Ernaux starts out memorializing father and mother equally, but it is the mother (the mother that lives on in her) whose imprint is most enduring. Mary Gordon and Alison Bechdel are more equal in attributing influence to both parents. In their cases, as in all others, the past and present of the other parent and the self keeps cropping up, intertwined in ever-changing patterns.

Mary Gordon starts the chapter "My Mother and My Father":

> They should never have married. Anyone could have seen they were wrong for each other, and everyone did see it; almost no one would have told them that marrying would be, for either of them, a good idea. They flew in the face of everyone's advice, of every imaginable branch of wisdom. Of course it didn't work.
>
> (2007:161)

She continues to write of their ups and downs, her memories of them together and apart, then concludes:

> But in the end we buried the body of my mother beside the body of my father, I came to understand it was only right. They were, after all, husband and wife.
>
> (185)

Parents who were "wrong for each other" are more frequently portrayed than those who lived happily ever after. Alison Bechdel is another writer who centers one book about each of her parents: their mismatch caused by his closeted gay life, a marriage that ended with an automobile accident—deemed a probable suicide—when an affair became public and her mother asked for a divorce.

In *Fun Home: A Family Tragicomic*, a graphic memoir, Bechdel traces the formation of her own lesbian identity through her relationship with her father. The man who had always pushed her to be more feminine is found in photos that clearly establish his womanly bent. "He's wearing a woman's bathing suit. A fraternity prank? But the pose he strikes is not mincing or silly at all. He's lissome, elegant."

She goes on to compare a photo of him at age twenty-two with one of herself at twenty-one. She remembers that hers was taken by a lover and wonders if his was too. She places the pictures side by side so we can see: "The exterior setting, the pained grin, the flexile wrists, even the angle of shadow falling across our faces—it's about as close as a translation can get" (120).

I like Bechdel's use of the word "translation." Whether writing of mother or father, the authors do not so much identify with their parents as attempt to translate their lives into their own language, their own lives.

Adding to the difficulties of "translation" from our parents' lives to ours is the passage of years that can obscure as well as edify.

Lynne Sharon Schwartz observes:

Indeed my father, who was such a vivid presence for me in his lifetime, after his death began fading like a Polaroid photo going in the wrong directions, from color and definition back to milky blur. I once thought I knew him through and through, each atom; I had studied him with critical scrutiny, as daughters do. Now I'm not sure I knew anything at all except the surface. Now, unless I make a conscious effort to locate the particles of him that lodged in me, he's like someone I used to see around all the time but never knew very well. Certain people need to be physically present in order to be fully apprehended. My mother remains as vivid as when I last saw her alive. I know her better now than I did then.

(2009:153)

Again, an author's phrase, "particles of him that lodged in me," sets me on a reverie.

I pick up the phone on a Saturday morning in November to hear the voice of my father's daily helper. "He's gone." She had let herself in and found him still in bed, "gone." His bed was usually rumpled after a restless night but he was peaceful, on his side, not a crease in the sheets. I cling to that detail; death came swiftly, painlessly.

We were not religious, and the rabbi found by the funeral home did not know us. It was not yet customary for family members and friends to speak at funerals, so I prepared something for him to read: the poem "My Father Moved Through Dooms of Love" by e. e. cummings. My favorite line, "Joy was his song," said it all, but I felt the need to say more. I wrote a few paragraphs, each beginning, "Who was Bob Burack?" I continued, "Ask . . . ," listing all the people whose lives he touched, from the closest friend to the chance encounter with the drugstore cashier. My wish was to show him as all of a piece.

I did not ask myself then, so now I do; now I answer. Who was Bob Burack? A man who made his daughter feel pretty and smart—so pretty and smart that by the time she was old enough to realize that she was far from the fairest or brightest in the land, it no longer mattered. A man who coped as best he could through a difficult forty-nine-year marriage. A man who barely made it through the seventh grade and couldn't set foot in a library because "it smells like a school in there!" A song and dance man who taught me to be the straight man in vaudeville skits. A man who was fine-tuned to see the humor in everything and the good in everyone. Mark Twain with a Boston accent. Milton Berle with a smelly cigar. A salesman by trade and by nature with a salesman's gift of words, of empathy, of persuasion.

I have not found my father's like, or the relationship between us, in any of the works I read. I see myself and my mother everywhere.

Many of the authors seek out ways they are or are not their mothers. Like Rich, they speak to a generational difference in the roles and opportunities open to women; mothers who were denied the education or life choices open to their daughters, mothers with limited lives, stifled desires. Like Ernaux they note the distance they have come from "the legacy" as well as its inescapable pull.

The conflict is most often cited in serious terms. A humorous take is rare but, when it does occur, all too recognizable. In "Travels with My Mother," Terry Castle—a feminist academic in her early fifties, young enough to be the daughter of most of the authors—describes a holiday trip to Santa Fe with her eighty-two-year-old mother:

Despite fifty years of walking and talking on my own, I realize I'm already starting to devolve, to morph back, as if inexorably, into that hungry, unkempt, much-loathed thing: My Mother's Daughter. All the familiar insecurity is surging back up in me, along with the lower-middle-class family mania—seemingly inbred in both of us—for talking endlessly and anxiously about what things are "nice" or "not nice." Infantilization hardly encompasses it. Even as we trundle from boutique to boutique I find myself reflexively chirping back my mother's aesthetic verdicts, in part (I tell myself) to make her feel secure in a strange place, in part for the simple reason that I am becoming disoriented. We're like a mother-daughter ventriloquist-dummy team, only one in which the ventriloquist, for some odd reason, is sitting in the dummy's lap. Delivered thrillingly yet forcefully, over the shoulder, Mavis's opinions become my opinions as I push her along, my wooden jaws—loosely secured by pegs—start clacking up and down in a strange parody of the maternal speech. She's sitting down but leading the way. I'm getting blurry by comparison.

(2010:141)

In a sense "Travels with My Mother" is an apt title for all the authors—whatever their ages. The mother outside and the mother inside are always present.

Nancy K. Miller, another contemporary academic, writes:

My mother lives in my pockets and also in my face. In the mirror, I silently measure with her the spreading pores, the advancing crepe, lines that crease even earlobes, I think: In fifteen years I, too, could be dead. Of course that doesn't tell me what I need to know. How to live with this face—our face—in the face of death. How to live without that other against whom we think we know who we are.

(2002:68)

The mother, "the other against whom we think we know who we are," becomes the measuring rod against which we measure our own lives. When the mother's life is unfulfilled, they are taken into the self; anger and resentment battle with compassion, sorrow, and regret. I read on, remembering Polly, my mother.

Marge Piercy writes:

I treasure many photographs of others, especially those of my parents when they were young or when they were not so young but I was. I have written poems about some of these photographs. Whenever I look at the few pictures of my mother in her youth that I possess, my sense of how she was cheated of her potential, how she stymied and stifled and starved of affection and pleasure and knowledge, cuts through me. I mourn her death but I also mourn her stunted and unfulfilled life. I resemble my mother more as I age than I did when I was younger. Sometimes when I see a particular photograph now, that resemblance will startle and touch me.

(2001:152)

And Simone de Beauvoir:

I talked to Sartre about my mother's mouth as I had seen it that morning and about everything I had interpreted in it—greediness refused, an almost servile humility, hope, distress, loneliness—the loneliness of her death and of her life—that did not want to admit its existence. And he told me that my own mouth was not obeying me any more: I had put Maman's mouth on my own face and in spite of myself, I copied its movements. Her whole person, her whole being, was concentrated there, and compassion wrung my heart.

(1973B:37–38)

Vivian Gornick notes the effect on her of her mother's lifelong clinging to an idealized image of her brief marriage and her inability to move beyond it after her husband's early death. Of the lasting imprint of the childhood mother on her psyche, she writes:

After Hiroshima dead bodies were found of people who had been wearing printed kimonos when they were killed. The bomb had melted the cloth on their bodies, but the design on the kimonos remained imprinted in the flesh. It seemed to me in later years the deep nerveless passivity of that time together had become the design burned into my skin while the cloth of my own experience melted away.

(1988:128)

I feel that imprinted design of my parents on my own body—even as I wonder, along with so many authors, what went so wrong with our mothers' lives and why.

Margaret Drabble writes a book about jigsaw puzzles, a pastime that she turns to in times of despair—but the depth of that despair cannot be kept out of it.

> My mother's angry depression seemed to me to be clearly related to her inertia and frustration, which affected so many educated and half-educated women of her generation; if she'd had more to do, if she hadn't had so much domestic help, if she'd been able to pursue a career, if she'd been more active, if she'd gone out for walks, things might have been different.
>
> (2009:171, 172)

I am moved by all the entries but break down only when reading about Anne Roiphe's mother, whose wedding picture appears in the book's unnumbered centerfold, with the following caption:

> Blanch Roth in wedding gown, on the day of—too late. What beautiful silk, what beautiful lace, what stillness of the fingers in her lap. If only I had been there I would have held her hand and kissed her face and calmed her nerves. Is the picture lying? Was she so beautiful a bride or am I a partisan who finds her all-white moment so gorgeous that it verges on the cruel.

And within the book itself:

> Our mother was afraid if she bought a dress it was the wrong color, the wrong style. She would take it back and buy another.... She was quite sure that she herself was unqualified for what might be expected.
>
> (1999:28)

That fear of being judged and found wanting; that is the Polly I remember, the Polly who lives within me, the Polly I have defined myself in opposition to even as I weep for the years she lost to illness and despair.

In the last year of her life, Polly could have been called "the madwoman in 3C"; a bald, ranting, manic-depressive barbiturate addict whose agony spilled over into the halls. There was anger at the ruckus, commiseration with the aides, pity for my father and me, but mostly an unspoken wish for it all to be over. At the news of her death, mute neighbors merely nodded condolences; there were simply no words. But one woman tried. "Your mother . . . ," she began, faltered, and finally said: "your mother . . . was a lady." And restored my mother's essence to me, along with her frequent quoting of an adage of *her* childhood: "A lady will always do and say the kindest thing in the nicest way."

Even in extremis, Polly had the ways of a lady about her. And if the polished sterling pickle fork and sugar tongs were too much, the good manners, the handwritten notes (in a hand identical to my own), an innate well of integrity, graciousness, and courtesy were not.

Polly was a victim many times over: errant genes, belittling parents, doctors who fed her addiction, the roles of midcentury wife and mother that fit so uncomfortably about her. Her aspirations were modest: to keep a well-running house, to entertain with style, to raise a child who would grow up to do the same. Still they always felt beyond her reach. She viewed each day as a burden and was constantly scornful of my father's happy outlook. "Life isn't singing and dancing," she would say.

She recalled the best days of her life as taking place before her marriage, before me: summer days on the beach in Nahant, studying piano at the New England conservatory, learning typing and Gregg shorthand at "business school," and working in an office until she married. She was determined that I learn this skill—extolling the pleasure of copying down the boss's words in code and giving them back all neat and centered on the page. I was a rebellious sixteen. "But they're not *your* words." She didn't know what I was talking about, but at that very moment, I did.

I wonder what Colette and Maya Angelou would think of each other. They are women of different centuries, countries, races, lives, but, after immersion in their writing, I see them as inspirational soul sisters. Each has made peace with her memories and helped me find peace in mine.

Maya Angelou thinks aloud at her mother's deathbed:

> "You were a terrible mother of small children, but there has never been anyone greater than you as a mother of a young adult." I looked at my mother's form and thought about her passion and wit. I knew she deserved a daughter who loved her and had a good memory, and she got one.
>
> (2013:224)

Could it be that love and a memory that encompasses the good and bad may be all it takes?

Colette begins *Break of Day* with the reproduction of a letter written by her mother to Colette's second husband:

> Sir. You ask me to come and spend a week with you, which means I would be near my daughter, whom I adore. . . . All the same I'm not going to accept your kind invitation, for the time being at any rate. The reason is that my pink cactus is probably going to flower. It's a very rare plant I've been given, and I'm told that in our climate it flowers only once every four years. Now I am already a very old woman, and if I went away when my pink cactus is about to flower, I am certain I shouldn't see it flower again. So I beg you sir, to accept my sincere thanks and my regrets, together with my kind regards.

And continues:

> Whenever I feel myself inferior to everything about me, threatened by my own mediocrity, frightened by the discovery that a muscle is losing its strength, a desire its power or a pain the keen edge of its bite, I can still hold up my head and say to myself: "I am the daughter of the woman who wrote that letter."
>
> (1961:5)

Colette could have interpreted the letter as rejection. (What devoted mother would prefer waiting around to see a flower bloom to visiting a daughter she rarely sees?) Instead, she turns it into an affirmation of the self she has become. Can I do the same?

I am the daughter of Polly and Bob Burack. Like Polly, I always try "to be a lady." I often fail. I have her face and her handwriting but not her musical gift. I don't keep house or entertain as well as she (in her best days) did, but I do it more often, with greater pleasure and less anxiety. I touch type as rapidly as she did. The words that land on the page are my own.

Like Bob, I am a salesman—not of women's apparel but of ideas. (For what is teaching and writing if not salesmanship?) The education he scorned is my delight: the smells of library and school as redolent as a bakery. I have his sense of humor, his ease with strangers, his confidence that things will all work out for the best. I have learned that life *is* singing and dancing.

The authors helped me see that the pieces don't need to fit, or make sense, or ever tell the whole story. Fragments from their lives remind me of fragments of mine—and that is enough.

I think, not for the first time, that there has to be a statute of limitations on how one's mother and father failed as people or as parents. For here we are, containing parts of them that we have built on, and continue to build on as long as we live. It is enough to say, "I am the daughter of the woman . . . ," "I am the daughter of the man . . . ," and continue writing our own stories.

6

THERE IS A GRACE IN
DEATH, THERE IS LIFE

Grief is at the heart of the human condition. Much is lost with death, but not everything. Life is not let loose of lightly, nor is love. There is a grace in death. There is life.

—KAY REDFIELD JAMISON, *NOTHING WAS THE SAME: A MEMOIR*

I KNEW that I would be a widow. I had even thought about what I might do when the time came. There were those trips to Europe Roy was no longer up to making, daylong events in the city that he now found too tiring. Every adventure ended with my coming home to tell him about it. Roy would be gone but somehow still here.

We hadn't needed the tests that uncovered silent heart attacks and mini strokes, following the "moderate" stroke ten years before, to tell us where the constant fatigue and obvious slowing down were headed. We had developed a bit of a routine about it. Roy would say, "I'm ready." I would say, "I'm not." He would say, "You'll be fine." I would not answer. We'd go on to talk about tomorrow.

And not metaphorically. That Friday, just before I left for a home visit to an ailing client, we planned for Saturday; a trip to a specialized store to see if we could find the right bulb to salvage an antique lamp and a visit to a Chelsea gallery that had just opened a promising show. When I returned two hours later to find that he had died and collapsed—half undressed—onto the bed I did not think: How could this happen? How will I live without him? I thought: How lucky! He had decided to turn in early and Death caught him in an instant, exactly as he would have wished. Without pain. Without having to undergo the frailty and dependence he most feared. I was happy for him, as if he had pulled some sort of a coup.

He had told me I'd be fine, so I believed him. I *was* fine with the EMT crew, with the police, with the children, family, and friends, and with all the arrangements that had to be made.

It was a few days before I began to shake and sweat. I woke myself up at night calling "help" and "come back." I got up in the morning with a stomach knotted in pain. I stopped eating and lost fifteen pounds I could not spare. I walked ten miles a day up and down city streets, sobbing behind dark glasses, until I fell, resulting in a bone bruise that turned my left leg black from knee to ankle and had me limping for the next two months.

From the time I was twenty years old, his life had been entwined with mine. Now the twine had broken and a part of me had fallen away.

Joyce Carol Oates wrote: "For when Ray was alive, even when he wasn't with me I was never alone: now that Ray is gone, even when I am with other people, a crowd of other people, I am never not-alone" (2011:236).

Roy was so . . . gone. His absence filled all the spaces he was not. In his last months I would go out far more often than he. I enjoyed the time alone. During long walks or at lectures he was no longer up to making, the shadow of his former self accompanied me. I would store up details to come back and tell him. Returning to the loft, climbing the stairs, I hoped to find him at the computer (he was working, feeling OK!); next best, sitting in a chair reading the paper (he was not up to working but feeling good enough to concentrate); lying on his back on the bed, dozing (not good at all). Still, even then, he would raise himself at the sound of my entry, smile, and ask about what I'd been up to.

I opened a Letters to Roy file on my computer. Early letters echoed early dreams in which he disappeared without an explanation, without a forwarding address—leaving me, for the first time in fifty-four years, alone, filled with questions: Where am I to go? What am I to do? I wrote as if it were an attachment to affix to an email—to one of the far-off places I dreamed he was in, on a secret mission and unable to get word to me.

It is hard for me now to decipher all those early letters; incoherent in some places, filled with hasty typos in others.

About eight months later, I had a different dream. I was on a crowded city street and someone called "the lawyer is coming." I looked for my current lawyer—Roy's colleague who helped me through those hard days after the death. But no, it was Roy himself! Handsome, and striding purposefully as he had in the prime of life. "See," I said to the people around me. "He was cremated but he didn't need his body to come back!" We found a quiet place and made love. All the old feelings returned. I wanted it to go on forever. Then, suddenly, I pictured a class of students waiting for me. There was no way to get word out to them. It was hard to break away but I had no choice. Roy understood. I awoke with the feel of his body still on mine.

I continued to make entries to the file—though they became shorter and less frequent as time passed. Reading it over, I note that after that dream my letters were calmer. There were fewer typos and the sentences that had been choppy and disjointed were clearer. The style also changed. It became more of a journal or log than a letter. I was no longer talking to him but to myself.

Kay Redfield Jamison's memoir, from which I took this chapter's title, is one of a group of "first year as a widow" books that have come out during the past decade. Jamison joins Joan Didion, Joyce Carol Oates, and Anne Roiphe in charting the moments from death of a husband to a time twelve months hence, echoing long-held conceptions of an appropriate time of grief as well as the more recent publisher's interest in the year as time enough to assimilate a new experience and share the news, as seen in several "A Year of . . . " book titles. There is a sense of experiment that seems more appropriate for living in Provence or living biblically than living without a life partner. Maybe not. Perhaps the narrative structure of beginning, middle, and end is just the thing—the "year" represents a process that calls for a temporal representation.

I have read each of the four memoirs twice—once when I was in the dark pit of grief and now that I sit down to write of the experience. The first readings were disappointing. Some made me angry and I talked back. "What difference does it matter Why he died?" I asked Didion. "Why are you doing all the research *now*?" "Why are you going out with these men who don't know, or appreciate, all you are?" I asked Roiphe. "It can only make you miss your husband more." Of course, the conversations said more about me than about them. I completely overlooked the differences between their situations and mine, as well as the stylistic and storytelling approaches they brought to the task.

On second reading I bypassed the particularities and cut to the chase— not to the beginning of the end, but the end of the beginning—where the authors are after the year ends and they go on with their lives.

I try to place myself in their midst, to find insights from their experiences that illuminate my own.

Once again, Joan Didion stands out from the crowd; the lilting beauty of her writing belying its message:

> I did not want to finish the year because I know that as the days pass, as January becomes February and February becomes summer, certain things will happen. My image of John at the instant of his death will become less immediate, less raw. It will be something that happened in another year. My sense of John himself, John alive, will become more remote, even "mudgy" softened, transmitted into whatever best serves my life without him.
>
> (2005:225–26)

She goes on to advise:

> Let them become the photograph on the table.
> Let them become the name on the trust accounts.
> Let go of them in the water.

And concludes:

> Knowing this does not make it any easier to let go of him in the water.
> In fact the apprehension that our life together will decreasingly be the center of my every day seemed today on Lexington Avenue so distinct a betrayal that I lost all sense of oncoming traffic.

I do not feel betrayal at going on with my life, nor do I feel that I must relinquish my dead. Then I remember that this is the Didion whose memoir of her early years in New York is titled *Goodbye to All That*. She seems to believe that life's experiences consist of discrete units; one door must close before another can open. The dead can be either at the center of your life or all but forgotten.

In fact, Didion's view is not unique—it was first put forth by Freud (1917) in his seminal work *Mourning and Melancholia* and accepted by mental health professionals for close to half a century. The theory, in brief, posits that we each have a finite amount of psychic energy to affix ("cathect") to others ("objects") in our lives. If we are to move on after the death of the object, we must "decathect"—unhinge the energy so it can attach itself elsewhere.

By the time I started training in the early 1970s, Freud's view had been overtaken by the premise of Elisabeth Kübler-Ross's book *On Death and Dying* (1969). She originated the idea that mourning follows a series of "stages." The stages are a sequential progression from shock and disbelief, through denial, anger, bargaining, and ending with acceptance—each of which must be mastered before proceeding to the next. The Kübler-Ross formulation became so much a part of the popular culture that it endures to this day despite professional criticism that arose almost immediately.

The first criticisms spoke to the failure to individualize the person or situation: the scheme does not account for such differentials as illness, mode of treatment, environmental context, ethnicity, or life-style of the individual. As the decades passed, subsets of mourning received attention. Mental health clinicians learned of "complicated grief," which resists resolution because of unresolved feelings about the deceased, and "disenfranchised grief" (Doka 1989), which occurs when the mourner's relationship with the deceased is unrecognized or devalued. Also observed was a difference in mourning styles: some individuals are seen as "affective" in their responses while others are "instrumental" (Doka 1989). And theorists continue to identify variables: age, gender, relationship, inherent personality patterns, and culture are seen as having an influence. Most significantly, all have come to believe that not only is it possible for the dead to continue to live on within us; it may be necessary. Often the discontinuity of death can be healed *only* by a continuity of feeling (Gilbert 2005; Konigsberg 2011).

It is a view that finds confirmation in Jamison:

> Over time, solace more than pain came from my memories of Richard. Thoughts of him were sweeter, less often jagged, stabbing things. There is a time limit to grief, I began to understand. Grief will end. I am alive. I love Richard, but I love life as well. Grief was beginning to wear out its welcome. "But though this has been a day and night of much trouble," wrote William Bradford, "yet God gave them a morning of comfort and refreshing." Life was on the other side of grief, morning on the far side of a hard night.
>
> (2009:190)

Jamison does not write, "I loved Richard." She writes, "I love Richard," and goes on, "but I love life as well."

And in a practical voice, Roiphe continues with what that life might look like, summing up a view that meets my own:

> I will be sad often but not always. I will be lonely most always but not unbearably so. I will look forward to small things: a dinner with friends, a movie, the first orange persimmons. I will miss sex. I will miss conversations past midnight with the cover pulled up tight across the chest to keep the warmth inside while cold air frosts the windowpanes. I will have no one to tell good news or bad. I will miss the unsaid things that passed between H. and me. But I will manage without them. I will make new friends in unexpected places. I will take a trip somewhere I have always wanted to go. I will not let grief become my constant companion. I will refuse its offer to accompany me to the corner, to the night, to the next month.
>
> (2008:213–14)

And it is in Joyce Carol Oates that I find validation of my own refuge in work—teaching that is such a wholehearted, whole-minded, whole-bodied endeavor that whatever one is feeling stops at the classroom door:

I am gladly relieved to be teaching! To be back in the presence of under-graduates who know nothing of my private life. For two lively and two absorbing hours I am able to forget the radically altered circumstances of this life—none of my students would guess, I am certain, that "Professor Oates" is a sort of raw bleeding stump whose brain, outside the perimeters of the workshop, is in thrall to chaos.

(2011:172)

Some critics cited the fact that Oates remarried before her book's pub-lication as invalidating her claim of deep grief. I am not among them. I see the act as affirmation of the individuality of each loss, the validity of each response.

Just recently I came upon two works that speak to where I am now—four years after Roy's death. The first comes from Madeleine L'Engle's journal:

Does a marriage end with the death of one of the partners? In a way, yes. I made my promises to Hugh "til death us do part" and that is what has happened. But the marriage contract is not the love that builds up over many years, and which never ends, as the circle of our wedding band never ends. Hugh will always be part of me, go with me wherever I go, and that is good because despite our faults and flaws and failures, what we gave each other was good. I am who I am because of our years together, fed by his acceptance and love of me.

(1988:230)

I, too, was "fed" by Roy's acceptance and love. We met when I was twenty and he was twenty-four. Today, many young men and women of those ages have a wealth of world and sexual experience behind them. We had neither. We were truly innocents with no idea of what life was about or what it might ask of us. We became who we were as individuals because of the strengths we gained from each other.

The second comes from M.F.K. Fisher—whose sexual dream is akin to my own. She writes about *les vendangeuses*—a wildflower that blooms near vineyards at the same time the grapes are ready to pick. They now fill vases throughout her house, and she writes that to her, they are Timmy (her second husband and the love of her life), who died decades before.

> Perhaps it is because I am quite old by now, into my seventy-sixth year, but I know that I am completely alive sexually for this man who died more than forty years ago.... I feel passionately aware of Timmy, more so than for a long time, and it is because of my new awareness of these strong little weeds.... So now I am an old woman and I think passionately but with a partly cautious deliberative detachment of the man I love. I'll never lie with him again, and feel him within me, but I'm thankful that I still have the memory so strongly always, and that the little sturdy flowers have brought it again to me. Dreams and half-conscious stirrings of strong sexual awareness do not bother me at all, and all I can hope is that other people may know some of them too, as happily as I do. I have no desire to bring them to any culmination, perhaps because they have already been fulfilled to my full capacity.
>
> (1995:156–57)

As the years pass, Roy retains a special place in my pantheon of the dead but, in truth, has joined all those beloved others who died before and after him: the grandmothers who died when I was in my thirties, the parents, aunts, uncles, and mentors who died when I was in my forties, fifties, and sixties. The friends who have died since. By the time we reach our seventies, the crowd around us is thin. So many who filled our thoughts and days are now gone.

Simone de Beauvoir was sixty-five when she enumerated the types of loss and their consequences to the survivor in her typical reasoned, cause-and-effect fashion. A presentation devoid of the tangle of human emotion until, in its last sentences, she breaks down to face the experience of loss in her own life.

> When it is our elders who die, then it is our own past that they carry away with them. There are people in their sixties who suffer, when they lose friends or relatives of their own generation, from the loss of a certain image of themselves that the dead possessed: with him there vanishes a part of youth or

childhood that he alone remembered. And for the old, it is a never-ending grief to lose those who are younger than themselves and whom they associate with their own future, above all if they are their children, or if they have brought them up: the death of a child, of a small child, is the sudden ruin of a whole undertaking; it means that all the hopes and sacrifices centered upon him are pointless, utterly in vain. The death of friends of our own age does not possess the character of bitter failure; but it does wipe out the relationship we have had with them. When Zaza died, I was too intent upon the future to weep for my own past; I wept only for her. But I remember my distress, much later, at the death of Dullin, although indeed he and I had never been really intimate. It was a whole section of my life that had collapsed.

(1973A:545)

How are we to live with whole sections of our lives collapsed? Colette—her stubborn, indomitable self—simply refuses to do so:

In my heart of hearts I blame them for dying, calling them careless, imprudent. How could they deprive me of their company, and so abruptly, how could they think of doing such a thing to me! So I have banished from sight and mind the vision of them lying prone and lifeless forever. Fargue turned suddenly to stone? I'll have none of it. My Fargue is still wearing his dusty walking-shoes, still talking, scratching the head of his black cat, is still ringing me up, still tramping from Lipp to Menilmontant and berating his bed for its too maritime blue. . . . Marguerite Mreno's feet still shod with static gold? Certainly not! They live in my memory as they were: wayward, restless, vulnerable and never tired.

(1963:9)

My current dreams of Roy, of my parents, of recently departed friends have a common theme. I no longer think of them as far away. They are living within walking distance, and I have been neglecting them. How could I not have seen them for so long? Surely they must be needing something from me, thinking I have forgotten them? I try to get through to them, but all efforts fail. I can't remember their phone numbers. The building front has changed and I can't find my way to the front door. As I awaken and realize they are dead, I am flooded with conflicting emotions. Anguish turns to relief as I learn that I was not at fault.

Reading on, I find how close our reactions to death are to our reactions to life. It is like Didion to need the finality of closing a door. It is like Colette to see the death as a personal affront and refuse to accept it. Just as it is like me to turn the tables on abandonment—my dead have not abandoned me, I have abandoned them.

Just as it is like Maya Angelou to convert her anger about death into a lesson on how to live:

> I am besieged with painful awe at the vacuum left by the dead. Where did she go? Where is she now. . . . There is, always, lurking quietly, the question of what certainty there is that I, even I, will be gathered into the gentle arms of the Lord. . . . I find surcease from the entanglement of questions only when I concede that I am not obliged to know everything. In a world where many desperately seek to know all the answers, it is not very popular to believe, and then state, I do not need to know all things. I remind myself that it is sufficient that I know what I know and know that without believing that I will always know what I know or that what I know will always be true. Also, when I sense myself filling with rage at the absence of a beloved, I try as soon as possible to remember that my concerns and questions, my efforts and answers should be focused on what I did or can learn from my departed love. What legacy was left which can help me in the art of living a good life.
>
> (1993:47)

The more I read a variety of old women, writing of their beloved dead, the deeper my understanding of the meaning of Angelou's "legacy." Beyond memories, beyond lessons to be learned, or the sure knowledge we will join our dead before long, is the realization that they live on, within us.

May Sarton captures the day-to-day nature of their continuing presence:

> When I plant bulbs I pat the earth around each one and realize suddenly that that is what my mother did. I never cook carrots without remembering

thyme, a little onion, and sugar as Celine used to do, or make my bed without a vivid recalling of Grace Dudley's insistence on hospital corners as we stretched a sheet taut between us; when I take my father's cane on a walk with my dog I find myself striding along as he did . . . on the rare occasions when I drink a martini the image wells up of the square cut-glass bottle with buffalo grass in it from which Kot poured gin for James Stephens and me. I see the reds among the fresh greens of spring with Quig's eyes. These are not conscious evocations nor very important in themselves, but it is their interweaving through every day that explains what influence truly is. We become what we have loved.

(1976:23)

Friday nights at 6 P.M. are still hard. Wherever the day or hour finds me, I replay our last hour together. Roy was seated at the computer when I left. Did I kiss him goodbye? I don't think so. I was in a rush and he was involved in a game of FreeCell. How he loved that game! What would have happened if I were there when he fell on the bed? The EMTs would have come sooner. His life might have been saved; most probably a diminished life he would not have wanted. He was ready. I was not. Did he somehow will himself to die just then, in that way, without me as a witness?

Or is it just a story I tell myself—a story like the dream of his second coming—constructed to calm me, to tell me that all was as it was meant to be; that he would approve of the life I am leading now.

I continue Letters to Roy on the computer, but their tone has changed. Once again, I write to him. Sometimes a month will pass without an entry. Then I write one a day for a week or so. On good days, I share news that he might find of interest. I inform him of what I have done and what I am about to do. On days when I feel frightened, anxious, or sad, I ask him to give me strength, to remind me that this too will pass. When I have a difficult decision to make—I set it all on the page and ask him to help me do the right thing. Reading over recent entries, I am amused to see that I use his style of reasoning: laying out the pros and cons with care, then going with my gut feeling.

Several widows I know remove the wedding band from their ring finger; one told me how she hates the term "widow" and that she wants to be seen as an independent single woman. I wear my ring because I still "have" my husband. My parents are dead, but I am still their daughter. I am still Roy's wife. He is no longer in an undisclosed location immune to my pleadings for return. He is within me. My inner voice is a blending of his voice and my own.

Waves of grief catch me by surprise. I might have predicted it was doing the things we always did together: old movies at the museum, lunch at our favorite restaurants. But it is at those times that I am most content; as if I am living the day with him. I miss him most when I start doing something new that he would have enjoyed that the tears well up. It is when they say "maestro to the pit" at the beginning of the HD opera. It is when an architecturally interesting building goes up in our neighborhood and he is not there to marvel at it. It is when I try a new recipe and he is not there to tell me what a wonderful cook I am.

Life goes on in unexpected, mostly satisfying, and sometimes joyous ways. In death, Roy has become all the ages he lived at once. He is as he was in the pictures scattered about the house: the twenty-six-year-old groom, the young father, the middle-aged grandfather, the old man snapped on an ID card entering a secured building. I am, as he predicted, fine.

7

MY MAP OF A PLACE

Here before me now is my picture, my map, of a place and therefore of myself,
and much that can never be said adds to its reality for me, just as much of its
reality is based on my own shadows, my invention.

—M.F.K. FISHER, *MAP OF ANOTHER TOWN*

How hard it is to draw maps of the places of my life! Harder than considering the changes age has wrought on my body. Harder than remembering the lives of my parents. Harder even than recalling the rush of comfort at hearing Roy's key in the lock. Perhaps it is because maps of place encompass all these at once. The places are gone. The invention continues.

My maps have addresses that once were as familiar as my own name. Now, though I sometimes struggle for a street number or zip code, they all return to me. Sometimes, awakening at 3 am and unable to return to sleep, I select a place I once lived in and mentally roam the premises, recalling the fixed positions of windows, walls, and floors and the placement of objects—large as the grand piano in the foyer, small as a china figurine on a knickknack shelf. There are no people in these recollections, nor need there be. Though many are long dead, the rooms where they lived, the chairs where they sat, the things that they touched, contain them.

It gives me particular pleasure to trace the objects I live with today back to their origins. The two small Japanese watercolors that hang on my bedroom wall are all that remain of the studio apartment I shared with Roy as a bride, newly arrived from a quiet suburb of Boston to New York City, living an unimagined life atop a butcher shop on Second Avenue. We had next to no disposable income, but the pictures were one of our first purchases. They verge on schlock—a house atop a stream in the shadow of a large mountain and a small man appear in each. In the spring scene, he is making his way across the bridge leaning on a stick. In the fall scene, the bridge is gone and he is navigating a boat with the same stick.

What were we thinking? Did the pictures hold some metaphorical significance or did they simply match the green and orange tweed of the sofa bed, our sole piece of furniture? I only remember what we were doing—making love as they watched over us, glaring street lights penetrating our shadeless windows and noise from the saloon next door to the butcher bouncing off the walls.

As I read the authors, I see that I am not alone. The need to say "I've been there and now I am here" seems a universal way of confirming our continued existence, and all that we carry from then into now.

In *Not Now, Voyager* (2009), Lynne Sharon Schwartz cites Xavier de Maistre's *Journey Around My Room* from 1790. She describes this as a two-hundred-page excursion through the author's mind—a guided tour from his bed to his chair, his desk, his window—that lets the mind rather than the body wander. Intrigued, I follow the reference to its source—Alain de Botton's *The Art of Travel* (2002)—and then to the Web, where I find that de Maistre's opus was written when he was under house arrest for dueling; he goes from object to object—each calling up recollections.

I understand the impulse behind his book in a visceral way. Surely Xavier de Maistre felt just as I do—how much easier it is to let the mind, rather than the body, do the traveling. No tickets or schedules, no borders, no passports. Thought is the one thing that remains free no matter what changes outside the head.

The freedom of thought, of time travel, is open to those of us not under house arrest. And like de Maistre, the authors (who may now be in what they think of as their final place on earth) construct memory maps of other places, other rooms. They offer me a guided tour that helps me see my own places in a new light.

Writing about first places—the places of their birth or earliest childhood memories—often appears in the authors' earliest published works and crops up in different genres throughout the years. However, it is typically in their fifties and sixties that they begin the life writing on place that gains momentum and reaches an apotheosis in old age—as *Last House*, the title of Fisher's final collection, frankly indicates.

The enduring imprint of the first place cannot be overstated. The authors redraw the maps throughout their writing lives. Whether they are translated into fiction (*The Sea Wall* by Marguerite Duras) or occupy some nether world that catalogers alternately file under "fiction" or "memoir (*My Mother's House and Sido* by Colette); whether romanticized, rebelled against, or, more commonly, rendered as an amalgam of impressions resisting interpretation, they carry the author's inimitable stamp of style and mode of reflection.

Edna O'Brien—whose memoir *Country Girl* resonates with the title of her first novel *Country Girls*—writes of the house in Ireland where she grew up and visits now that she is old: it is uninhabited, the land around it overgrown, and rumors abound on what it might become.

> But in the lambent light of that August evening, with the sun going down, a bit of creeper crimsoning and latticed along an upstairs window, the whole place seemed to hold, and would forever hold, for me, regardless of bungalows or a five-star hotel, the essence of itself, the thing that gave it the sacred and abiding name of Home.
>
> (2013:18)

Later in the memoir, she writes of the impact of that home on her work:

> When, much later, I wrote about my mother, that preoccupation with her had intensified so that she permeated all worlds—her mother was the cupboard with all the things in it, the tabernacle with God in it, the lake with the legends in it, the sea with the oysters and the corpses, a realm into which she longed to vanish forever.
>
> (68)

O'Brien shifts between the first person of life writing ("I wrote about my mother") and the third person of fiction ("her mother was") to describe her mother's influence on her earliest impressions of the world. Moving outward from familiar objects in the cupboard to what lies below the surface of the sea—she illuminates the lifelong influence of one's first place on earth.

In *My Mother's House* Colette writes:

> Both house and garden are living still, I know; but what of that, if the magic has deserted them? If the secret is lost that opened me to a whole world— light, scents, birds and trees in perfect harmony, the murmur of human voices now silent for ever—a world of which I have ceased to be worthy?
>
> (1953:6)

She goes on to recall her mother's cry at 6:30: "Where are the children?" And she concludes:

> Two are at rest. The others grow older day by day. If there be a place of waiting after this life, then she who so often waited for us has not ceased to tremble for the two of us who are yet alive.
>
> (10)

Colette's map, like O'Brien's, stirs me with its imagery, but I feel no identification. It is only when I read Mary Catherine Bateson that a fragment of memory erupts. Bateson, the daughter of anthropologists Margaret Mead and Gregory Bateson, recalls being handed an implement as a child and told, "This is what we call a fork" (1990:50).

What *we* call a fork! Reading these words, I picture myself seated in a raised chair facing the wall at the small white table in the first kitchen I ever knew, facing what I now know to be "a place setting." There is a salad fork atop a triangular napkin (point out) to the left of a child's plate divided into three small portions; to the right is a butter knife (blade in), directly atop of which sits a glass of milk.

I am being instructed in the matter of knives and forks. The fork is held in the left hand, curved side down, while the knife in the right hand cuts—after which the knife is returned to the rim of the plate, blade side in. The fork—curved side now up—is transferred to the right hand to carry the cut food to the mouth.

The message was clear: there is a one right way to do things, and people who do them any other way are wrong. A decade was to pass before I became aware that people in other parts of the world had different views. A decade more until craft fairs became popular and I was to see many handsome bracelets constructed out of twisted forks.

How could my experience in a suburb of Boston circa 1940 have anything to do with the Simone de Beauvoir's haute-bourgeois upbringing in France decades before? Then I read in *Memoirs of a Dutiful Daughter*:

> The world around me was harmoniously based on fixed coordinates and divided into clear-cut compartments. No neutral tints were allowed: everything was in black and white; there was no intermediate position between the traitor and the hero, the renegade and the martyr: all inedible fruits were poisonous; I was told that I "loved" every member of my family, including my most ill favoured great aunts.... Whatever I beheld with my own eyes and every real experience had to be fitted somehow or other into a rigid category: the myths and stereotyped ideas prevailed over the truth: unable to pin it down, I allowed truth to dwindle into insignificance.
>
> (1958:17)

Bateson expanded her first map of the world into a lifelong exploration of other ways of being. She was comfortable facing the unexpected, approaching what we might call "otherness" with unbiased curiosity. Simone de Beauvoir's rebellion against her upbringing infused a lifetime of philosophical and historical analysis.

As I read authors on their first homes, I consider what vestiges of my earliest orientation toward life live on in me. And recognize that over seventy years have now passed since my first lesson of the knife and fork and I *still* eat following the pattern of my earliest teaching! I know it is not the only way to handle a knife and fork. In fact, it is somewhat ridiculous to keep switching hands, especially when compared to the no-nonsense

European approach. Still I persist. Habits of thought and action laid down in childhood have a way of hanging on against all reason. An insight that forces me to confront the quality I least like in myself—a tendency to be judgmental, to think my way is the only right way—might well have had its beginnings at that small white table.

Still, it was not until I read Joan Didion's *Where I Was From* (2003), written when she was in her sixties, that I recognized fully how maps of past places become maps of present selves. Chapter 1, a history of the development of California, is filled with geography and topography: surveys, pictures, and quotes from diaries attest to the pioneer struggle to survive on the long road from east to west. Chapter 2 begins "I was born in Sacramento" and continues with personal history. Didion is a collector of objects and memorabilia, all of which are described at length—until the last pages of the memoir, when she realizes that her family and personal history have no meaning to her adopted daughter, Quintana.

> In fact I had no more attachment to this wooden sidewalk than Quintana did; it was no more than a theme, a decorative effect. It was only Quintana who was real. . . . Later it seemed to me that this had been the moment when all of it—the crossings, the redemption, the abandoned rosewood chests, the lost flatware, the rivers I had written to replace the rivers I had left, the twelve generations of circuit riders and county sheriffs and Indian fighters and country lawyers and Bible readers, the two hundred years of clearings in Virginia and Kentucky and Tennessee and then the break, the dream of America, the entire enchantment under which I had lived my life—began to seem remote.
>
> (219–20)

De Beauvoir shares Didion's notion of closing the door to a past that has no further relevance in her life. They write of the first place to rid themselves of it and move on. Other authors, like Colette and O'Brien, keep the door ajar, never quite leaving that first place they called home while continuously circling back to redraw the maps. I find myself in their company.

Maps drawn in the midpoint of the authors' lives are different. They speak to places of their own choosing. The ambivalent—sometimes idealized, sometimes resentful—feelings attached to the first home have disappeared. After all, the authors have made a conscious decision to sojourn in this place. They often write about what we now call "second homes"—places in which they stay for weeks or months, either with others or alone. Whether these places are characterized as spots of private tranquility, or of busyness in the midst of family and friends, the emotions attached are sanguine.

The map that Fisher refers to in the opening quote of this chapter introduces recollections of the town of Aix-en-Provence, where she (a Californian who found her palette and life career of food writing in France) lived for a time with two young daughters. I start at mention of the cafes along Cours Mirabeau. I too was there!

Forgotten are Mary Frances and her daughters. Remembered is that cold December day when I chose freezing outside with the natives over indoor comfort with the tourists. Or maybe not. My map, like hers, is an invention yet as real as real can be.

Midlife maps are as likely to be prosaic as metaphorical. In fact, it is the variety of maps that speak to the vitality of women in their prime. Several authors write of the places where they lived as young and midlife adults. Like Fisher, they have the freedom of movement that accompanies an open spirit and the finances to afford it. Unlike the cloud of their dependence on others that overhangs first and last places, midlife places reflect a sense of power, of agency to be carried forward.

Then there are the few who find the need for a change of scene in their fifties—time alone to reflect on their lives to date, to commune with nature, and to plan their futures.

Alix Kates Shulman was sixty-three when *Drinking the Rain* (1995)—a memoir of her fifties—was published. It tells of a summer alone in in her family's vacation house, "The Nubble," on an island in Maine. A time-out from being a wife, a mother, an adult child, a feminist activist, a time to reflect on where she is in life's trajectory and what to do next. Three sections—the island, the mainland, the world—serve as an extended metaphor.

Shulman relishes the solitude and joy in the sea's bountiful harvest, and the glories of nature all around her fill the first two sections. In the world, she extracts wider meaning for herself.

> I remember how long it took me when I began gathering mussels to see their predators, the green crabs that share their habitat—except when I went crabbing and became momentarily blind to mussels. Like the blindness that comes from too much light, mine came from the sheer intensity of my focus, the ardor of my wish. Not until I understood the inextricable connection between mussels and crabs was I able to see both crabs and mussels at once. Just so, now that I've discovered the island's connection to the world, I see it everywhere.
>
> (204)

> Spray my apple tree? Never! But to keep it alive? Sometimes extraordinary measures must be taken in matters of life and death. It's one thing to hold your faith when everything's going fine, but in this year of so many shattered certainties I don't know what to do. Naturally, I hope my tree will bear again, let me taste again the pies of yore; but as I struggle with this latest challenge to my preconceptions in my ceaseless negotiation with the given, I'm thinking not of fruit but of survival.
>
> (217)

Colette's trip to the Midi of France—described in *Break of Day* (1961)—is a similar venture. Although the texts are dotted with references to other people, the reader pictures the authors essentially alone with their thoughts.

Many more midlife memoirs resemble Fisher's—filled with the ebb and flow of family life. Most of these are written at a distance of years as the authors look back on the enduring effect of place on the changing nature of their relationships with others. In her introduction to the journal that covers the last year of her husband's life, Madeleine L'Engle describes the home that spans forty years of their life together:

Crosswicks is a symbol for me of family and community life, of marriage in general and my own marriage in particular. It stands staunchly on the crest of one of the Litchfield hills in the northwest corner of Connecticut and through the centuries has withstood the batterings of many storms— blizzards, hurricanes, even a tornado—of love anger, birth, death, tears, laughter.

(1988:3)

The notion of place as a symbol of the web of relationships that took place there turns up repeatedly.

In *Practicalities* (1987)—transcribed conversations in which the voice of the interlocutor is redacted—Marguerite Duras, well into old age, free associates on the subject of home:

I have this deep desire to run a house. I've had it all my life. There's still something of it left. Even now I still have to know all the time what there is to eat in the cupboard, if there's everything needed in order to hold out, live, survive. I too still hanker for a sort of shipboard self-sufficiency on the voyage of life for the people I love and for my child.

. . . In the house in the country, at Neauphle-le-Château, I made a list of all the things that ought to be always in the house. There were a few dozen of them. We kept the list—it's still there—because it was I who'd written it down. It still includes everything.... [The list in three columns follows; it begins with table salt and ends with insulating tape.] The list is still there, on the wall. We haven't added anything. We haven't taken to using any of the hundreds of new articles that have been invented in the twenty years since it was written.

(49–50)

Duras wrote that? Duras of *The Lover*? Duras of wild, fantastical love in far-away places? Wonderous contradictions of selves abound in writings of place!

Fisher had Aix. L'Engle had Connecticut. Duras had Neauphle-le-Château. I had Montauk. The house our family called home through every weekend and summers from 1974 (when I was a young mother and the children were twelve and fourteen) until its sale after Roy's death in 2011 (when I was an old widow and "the children" were, indisputably, middle aged).

The house looked like a child's first drawing of a house—even one by a child like Roy or me, who had grown up in city apartments. A large, rectangular box, a window in each quadrant, a red door in the center. It was not an easy sell. In the years of Roy's illness and my inertia, nature had reclaimed its own. The trees—growing up and out—nudged the deck. Moss covered the small apron of would-be lawn that separated us from the woods. Deer had found the one property in the area that was not out to get them. No invisible shields or electrified fences stayed their course.

Outside, the house looked the same as the day our family entered it. Soon after we moved in, Roy made a foot-high panel to nail along the bottom of the red door. In black lettering was the word H O M E—drawn from a stencil, accidentally smudged in the process—with the faintest shadow about the letters. Sort of a gothic Addams Family effect, commentary and benison in one.

Inside hadn't changed much either. The house was to be sold as what is known as a fixer-upper or handyman's delight. Our broker went one better. The ad he ran in the local newspapers occupied the same space as others on the page, but photo and text were different. The heading: "Like Challenges?" The photo: our house in winter. Among the proud houses flaunting architectural detail and park-like landscaping, our house stood like an orphan—naked, barefaced, gray. The ad before me, I wanted to shout: "The picture is not the whole story. Look at the front door!" The first things that the buyers, a young, childless couple, did was replace it. The new door was not solid wood like ours but a pattern of multiple glass panes.

I refuse to mourn the red door. Or the removal of the makeshift greenhouse in which Roy started plants from seed each spring. Or the tear-down of the bookcases that lined the walls of the den. Or the rosy, old brick of the fireplace now painted white. They live on in memory just as they were.

The range and complexity of emotions that accompany maps of first and midlife places give way to simplicity in descriptions of last homes. It is a time when the preoccupation with what it takes to transform a house (a structure with floor, ceilings, walls, and windows) into home (a place of comfort and refuge that expands beyond its walls to the natural and communal worlds surrounding it) that occupies the authors throughout their lives comes to fruition.

The first chapter of Maya Angelou's memoir *Even the Stars Look Lonesome* (1997) is titled "A House Can Hurt. A Home Can Heal." She concludes the chapter:

> This is no longer my house, it is my home. And because it is my home, I have not only found myself healed of the pain of a broken love affair, but discovered that when something I have written doesn't turn out as I had hoped I am not hurt so badly. I find that my physical ailments, which are a part of growing older, do not depress me so deeply. I find that I am quicker to laugh and much quicker to forgive. I am much happier at receiving small gifts and more delighted to be a donor of large gifts. And all of that because I am settled in my home. . . . My life and good fortune carry me around the world. However, when I am on a plane and the pilot announces, "Ladies and Gentlemen, we have begun our descent into North Carolina," my burdens lift, my heart is at ease, and a smile finds its way all the way across my face. I know that soon I will be in a car that will stop on a quiet street in Winston-Salem, and I will step out and be home again.
>
> (9–10)

As I look about the loft, what I expect and hope will be my last place, I am filled with the same sense of rightness as the authors. It does not matter if they are by the sea or in the mountains, in the city or the country. They feel that they are in a place that contains all they need until they die.

Coming to that decision is a confrontation with the self. What do I need around me to make me comfortable and secure?

Deciding on her retirement home in Maine, Doris Grumbach writes:

> Perhaps I am truly at home when I am at peace with myself, surrounded by the serenity that comes from the Cove, a quiet so deep I am able to hear the roar of the sea in my inner ear, to see in my mind's eye absent friends as

well as the dead I have loved, to taste on the buds of fantasy the great meals I am no longer able to digest, to restore the scraps of a quiescent past long buried in my memory by an overactive present.

(1993:297)

M.F.K. Fisher aptly named her final edited collection *Last House* (1995). (The house itself consists of three rooms built to her specifications.) Her first line: "It is very simple: I am here because I choose to be." She continues:

It is plain that creature comforts are an acceptable part of my choice to live here in my later years. Aside from them as well as because of them, I find this house a never-ending excitement. . . . I move about fairly surely and safely in my *palazzino* and water the plants on the two balconies. I devise little "inside picnics" and "nursery teas" for people who like to sit in the Big Room and drink some of the good wines that grow and flow in these northern valleys. I work hard and happily on good days, and on the comparatively creaky ones I pull my Japanese comforter over the old bones, on my big purple bedspread woven by witches in Haiti and wait for the never failing surcease. How else would I live where I live? It all proves what I've said before, that I am among the most blessed of women, still permitted to choose.

Fisher hits on what seems to be the essential element in satisfaction with one's last place: that it is a place of one's own choosing.

Marge Piercy sums it up:

We are tight-knit family of two humans and five cats who live far out to sea on the land we have made fertile among our gardens and our woods. This is our chosen home. It has taken me a long time to arrive here and dig in. These are my wanderings in search of a place where I could write and be myself and have what I consider necessary and what is not perhaps necessary but makes life good enough to endure the hard times. A place and time to write is a necessity, and love is a luxury, but I have spent a great many years searching for both. I am a stray cat who has finally found a good home.

(2001:11)

Years of making home visits to old clients in New York City have made me something of a connoisseur of last places. From barren single rooms to overstuffed apartments, from immaculately clean to incomprehensibly fetid living spaces, I drew the map of invention around the house I choose in which to live out my days. A curator with a minimalist perspective, I consign many objects from past places to closets and cabinets—each to wait its turn in a rotation that changes with my whim and the seasons.

This frigid winter day, three days from the solstice, I am warmed by whatever my eye encounters. From my first place, a brightly painted wooden parrot on a perch, suspended from the kitchen ceiling, that recalls the joke attached to my mother's name (does anyone now remember "Polly want a cracker"?). A wooden cutting board that my father made in woodworking shop a century ago hangs beneath it. From that first studio apartment: the Japanese men eternally caught between river and mountain. From Montauk, the wall lamps that Roy made from old wooden lathes, each, like the long-gone "Home" plaque on the door, carrying an imperfection that marks it as uniquely his. Before I leave the loft this evening, I click on my grandmother's marble lamp—at its base an intricately carved boy in cap and knickers, a small girl behind in an old-style dress resting her head on his shoulder. Above a rounded dome cracked with the years. It will welcome me home.

8

INTERESTED IN BIG THINGS AND HAPPY IN SMALL WAYS

In spite of illness, in spite even of the arch-enemy sorrow, one can remain alive long past the usual date of disintegration if one is unafraid of change, insatiable in intellectual curiosity, interested in big things and happy in small ways.

— EDITH WHARTON, *A BACKWARD GLANCE: AN AUTOBIOGRAPHY*

WHEN I first read Edith Wharton's words, I felt as if they were written for me. It was more than Wharton's authoritative tone or the cadence of the sentence that affected me. It seemed to sum up a whole philosophy of aging that I had yet to assimilate. For I am the "one" to whom Wharton refers; past the usual date of disintegration and remaining alive. She uses that gracious old word "sorrow" to describe my state. It is not "grief" or "mourning," time-limited responses to a specific event, that I often feel but a state of being, a low-level subduing of the spirit. It seems as if I am constantly hearing about another friend's illness or death, while facing a new health issue of my own.

Wharton's words are not a conclusion of her autobiography; they are an introduction. As we read of all she had been, done, and known, she wants us to remember that her life, though transformed by age, is still being lived in the present tense. She is not yet ready to call it a day.

Her life was far more noteworthy than mine; yet as I read I see that, like her, the years through my sixties were packed full of activity and relationships. I was enveloped in a thickly woven fabric of roles and responsibilities:

frayed edges as the years passed but the center intact. I had a sense of my life as consisting of various parts coming together to make a coherent whole—an identifiable self who worked and loved, who had certain preferences and distastes, who was connected to others in patterns that remained relatively stable over the years.

Disintegration of the body or loss of loved ones is not what threatens to tear the fabric of myself but the result of that tear. The threads that united the fragments of my personality into a coherent whole, a recognizable self, have grown slack. Most of the people who gave back images of who I was are no longer here—Roy, parents, mentors, friends—have passed on. I no longer have the opportunity, much less the energy, to "reinvent" myself. So I am left with bits and pieces of who I was to cobble together who I will now be.

Wharton qualifies "sorrow" with "archenemy," implying unending struggle. And it is the day-to-day struggle of meeting life's challenges without previous anchors of work or a life partner, without anyone bearing witness, without the caring presence of important others who have died, that makes it so difficult. Older now than Wharton at the date of her death, I read on—deconstructing her sentences in hopes that they will reveal the truth of my life to me.

"Unafraid of change." Didn't Wharton notice that change is as rapid in old age as it is in childhood? Could she really be unaware that change is almost always for the worse? Even with her vast network of support, her strong will and financial assets, it is hard to believe that she was not afraid. Yet she has me in thrall. I read on.

"Insatiable in intellectual curiosity." Here Wharton is ahead of her time. Every professional and lay article on "successful aging" of today preaches taking on new mental challenges as a way of forestalling cognitive decline. Learn a new language! Take up tai chi! The neuroscientists tell us that construction of new pathways in the brain is possible if only we turn from the familiar to the new—a virtual calisthenics of the mind.

As I think of the authors I have read, it does not appear that they took on new mental challenges in old age. Just the opposite. They dig deeper into the well of who they were, what they knew, what they could do well.

Would Fisher have thought: "Enough food writing on assignment! Let me now explore the possibility of a journal about my daily life"? Would Sarton have said: "I am curious about how dictating my thoughts rather than writing them down will influence my style"? More likely, changes were an adaptation to their waning powers than a breaking of new ground.

What I read is not insatiable curiosity about new worlds but insatiable desire to continue the old worlds; to be as much as possible the people they were doing what they have always done—communicating their thoughts to themselves and to the world. In fact, it was the desire to continue that opened them to new ways of doing so.

"Interested in Big Things and Happy in Small Ways." Wharton doesn't define Big Things. The definition clearly differs from person to person. As I think about it, though, I imagine she was suggesting a turning away from the preoccupations of one's own life to an interest in affairs that occupy younger adults who are out and about in the world in a way I no longer am.

What with a changing physical self, sorrows over past losses, and fear of future losses—it is all too easy to turn inward. And it's not as if the outside world is exactly clamoring for the attention of the old. It is easy enough to let the world fend for itself, to retreat into a cocoon, and find comfort there.

I think of Marilyn French, a vocal proponent of the women's movement who was becalmed in old age. Near death from cancer, she finds peace in turning from the political to the personal in her life and writing:

> I am no longer driven. I no longer imagine that I can do much to help bring about the millennium of the humane ideal, or that I can change anything at all. I have relinquished my painful freight. I am free. I am permitted to enjoy myself. I have noticed that my laugh has changed, is more spontaneous, deeper. I am almost serene.
>
> (1998:255-56)

Reading French, I am reminded of how quickly I now get through my daily reading of the *New York Times*. I scan the stories of ghastly wars and mass shootings. Political updates are sufficient without the endless speculation of what might follow. I discard the sections on the latest trends in fashion or travel. I used to be surprised when the articles suggested things I thought everyone knew or couldn't imagine anyone wanting to know. I now tell myself, "They're not talking to you."

Then I recall Toni Morrison's speech, on receiving the Nobel Prize for Literature in 1993, about the fight for social justice and social good, and I reconsider.

> The old woman is keenly aware that no intellectual mercenary, nor insatiable dictator, no paid-for politician or demagogue; no counterfeit journalist would be persuaded by her thoughts. There is and will be rousing language to keep citizens armed and arming; slaughtered and slaughtering in the malls, courthouses, post offices, playgrounds, bedrooms and boulevards; stirring, memorializing language to mask the pity and waste of needless death. There will be more diplomatic language to countenance rape, torture, assassination. There is and will be more seductive, mutant language designed to throttle women, to pack their throats like pate-producing geese with their own unsayable transgressive words; there will be more of the language of surveillance disguised as research; of politics and history calculated to render the suffering of millions mute; language glamorized to thrill the dissatisfied and bereft into assaulting their neighbors; arrogant, pseudo- empirical language crafted to lock creative people into cages of inferiority and hopelessness. . . .
>
> Be it grand or slender, burrowing, blasting, or refusing to sanctify; whether it laughs out loud or is a cry without an alphabet, the choice word, the chosen silence, unmolested language surges toward knowledge, not its destruction. . . .
>
> Word-work is sublime, she thinks, because it is generative; it makes meaning that secures our difference, our human difference—the way in which we are like no other life.
>
> (2002:201–3)

After I recover from the beauty of Morrison's sentiment on "word-work" on "unmolested language" to redress the injustices of the world, I try to apply it to my own meager efforts to convert words and action to a worthy purpose.

Being useful has always been important to me, as I reminded students lamenting the hard work and low pay of our profession: "You'll never go home after a day of practice wondering if what you did was worthwhile. Each day is an opportunity to do something useful for someone else. How many jobs provide that bonus?"

Long after I stopped teaching, I tried to practice what I preached. After 9/11 I signed up for the New York City Emergency Response Team and went through the training for mental health professionals. During Hurricane Irene, I served a twenty-four-hour shift in a shelter. A year later Superstorm Sandy came along, the need for volunteers was even greater, and I was physically not up to it. Watching it all unfold and being powerless to help was painful. It seemed unbearably selfish to be concerned only with my own well-being in the face of such need.

Less resigned than French, less fiery than Morrison, I try to create a bridge between their contrary views. Can I change the world? Can I change myself? Should I even try?

As I try to negotiate a new way of being that can encompass my former self with who I am now, as I take on a new role in society—that of an old woman who can't do all she used to do but still wants to do all she can— Madeleine L'Engle reminds me of value in the smallest acts of good we can manage. Though I do not share her religious orientation, her words are a balm.

> But neither was Jesus adequate to the situation. He did not feed all of the poor, only a few. He did not heal all the lepers, or give sight to all the blind, or drive out all the unclean spirits. Satan wanted him to do all this, but he didn't. That helps me if I felt that I had to conquer all the ills of the world I'd likely sit back and do nothing at all. But if my job is to feed one stranger, then the money I give to world relief will be dug down deeper from my pocket than it would be if I felt I had to succeed in feeding the world.
>
> (1977:140)

Thinking about my new relationship to the world, what Wharton would call "the big things," I recall my early days teaching the concept of role theory. (The theory refers to the ways in which social roles influence human interaction by prescribing what tasks individuals are deemed capable and/or responsible for performing. Role theory receives less attention these days but remains of interest as a gender issue [Dulin 2007]).

In the 1980s role theory was of gerontological interest because it posited that aging was a "role-less role" in which old people, unmoored from their previous identities, were adrift. To teach this concept, I gave each student in class a set of index cards, on each of which they wrote one of the roles they currently occupied: parent to young children, adult child of older parents, husband or wife, sister or brother, worker, student, and so on. They then projected themselves into old age—discarding or amending cards one by one. "Student" went first. "Worker" followed. Then "Adult Child." They retained the parent card while realizing that the role would be freed of its daily responsibility. They retained the spouse and sibling cards, realizing that this too was tenuous—depending on the longevity of another. And the busyness of their daily lives vanished. Just like that. The message was that the stripping of societal roles led to a diminishment of self that had to be replenished if old people were to retain a purpose in life.

Fast forward to today when the key concept at gerontological conferences—the answer to all manner of ills associated with aging—is "social interaction." New roles as students, volunteers, and mentors not only provide old people with activity but act against social isolation, which has been found in study after study to be correlated with physical and cognitive decline. The older adult with a rich social network fares better on every scale of successful aging.

In the personal sphere, we now have elevation of the grandparent role. (A frequently aired television advertisement for a rehabilitation center features the testimonial of an old woman who, after her stroke, feared she would never again be able to play with her grandchildren.) What if you don't have grandchildren? Or if playing with them is not your deepest wish?

Social interaction is often preached as an antidote to what gerontologists have long spoken of as the inevitable, if often subtle, process of "disengagement": from the concerns and activities of the larger society (Cummings and Henry 1961). Disengagement theory has been debated for decades. Reams have been written from a variety of points of view, the basic objection being that it is unclear which is cause and which is effect: does the old person pull away from society, or does society pull away from the old person?

The most compelling theory—which is to say the one that best defines what most of us observe among the old people we know—was continuity theory (Kaufman 1994). Continuity theory holds that people do not change their patterns of thought or action as they age but continue to approach life in the same way they always have.

Each theory touches on but does not plumb what I have learned from the authors. None of the authors asks whether attention should be focused inward or outward. And although they continue the practices and relationships of earlier lives as long as possible, it is not sufficient.

The authors appear to recognize that role retention, engagement, and continuity are hard won in the face of multiple losses. In fact, their writing points to the particular rewards of letting go of who they once were to become who they now are. As I reread their writing from youth to age, I see that the authors have somehow been able to identify the basic principles they lived by, extract them from their transient manifestations, and re-create them in late life.

Wharton did heroic war work in World War I. Colette, as well as Angelou, was in the musical theater. Scott-Maxwell was a Jungian therapist. Others spent earlier years writing poetry, plays, fiction, or reportage. When those roles ended, they were forced to confront the core of self—the inner self—that propelled them and turn it to new ends. The authors teach me that the inner self is independent of social role. You don't have to be anything to anyone. It is sufficient to be someone to yourself.

Morrison's old woman has seen the worst of life, and it has not caused her to lose faith in the possibility of a single life, even that of "the old woman" struggling toward the light. In this, she recalls the words of Nancy Mairs, who constantly examines her faith in the light of living with multiple sclerosis and depression:

In fact, the end is all we know for certain about the historical Jesus: "he died at the hands of the Romans as a rebel against their rule in Palestine." He didn't have a choice. He was *human*, remember. When you're human, you're human all the way. No calling a halt to the condition when things gets nasty: "Enough for me. I'll be off now, thanks." When you're human, you go through a lot, some bits nicer than others, and then—always, always, one way or another—then you die.

(1993:194)

Human all the way. Knowing that we lack certain choices, that life will be hard and then we'll die—at the same time as we try to live a life that exemplifies the ideals that underlie our individual lives, in our brief time here. This is a "big idea" if ever there was one.

Maya Angelou writes:

Many things continue to amaze me, even well into the sixth decade of my life. I'm startled or taken aback when people walk up to me and tell me they are Christians. My first response is the question "Already?" It seems to me a lifelong endeavor to try to live the life of a Christian. I believe that is also true for the Buddhist, for the Muslim, for the Jainist, for the Jew, and for the Taoist who try to live their beliefs. The idyllic condition cannot be arrived at and held on to eternally. It is in the search itself that one finds the ecstasy.

(1993:73)

The search for a new way to relate to the world and the struggle to live one's best life—whether or not done in the name of religion—are worthy goals. That they are just beyond reach provides something to strive for. Meanwhile we have to get through each day. And here "happy in small ways" becomes important.

Florida Scott-Maxwell and May Sarton count the ways. Like many ill and disabled women in their eighties, they don't get around much anymore. Their inner lives and the striving to remain and build on who they were take place mainly within four familiar walls.

Scott-Maxwell writes, of physical comfort:

The woman who has a gift for old age is the woman who delights in comfort. If warmth is known as the blessing it is, if your bed, your bath, your best-liked food and drink are regarded as fresh delights, then you know how to thrive when old. If you get the things you like on the simplest possible terms, serve yourself lightly, efficiently and calmly, all is almost well.

(1968:88–89)

"All is almost well." Scott-Maxwell knows that all will not be well, no matter how comfortable she is able to make herself. Yet simply recognizing the small pleasures she is able to obtain, she elevates them. And herself as well. For after all, it is she who has identified what she needs and arranged it.

May Sarton is also devoted to tailoring the small dimensions of home to her satisfaction. In the final journal written before her death at eighty-three, she writes:

Most of the time I am happy, learning a new kind of happiness for me which has nothing to do with achievement or even with creation. Each day I plan something I can look forward to. Today it may be ordering bulbs. I think of a letter I want to write today, perhaps to Norma, who sent me a charming valentine she had painted, blue and purple and truly romantic. And I will make out the March checks; I greatly enjoy making out checks and spending money in every possible way. This is not only true of my old age; it has always been true.

(1996:252)

What has always been true for me is the fun of trying out new foods. Time was that I would cook and Roy would bake. There was something special to exclaim about every night. Breads and fruit tarts were his specialty; soups and cheesy concoctions were mine. We savored old-time favorites but just as often were inspired by what looked good at the greenmarket that day. Without him, the dining room table lost its point. An apple or granola bar in the hand was enough. Time hardly seemed to move. Until, one day a month or so after he died, numb with grief, I flipped on the television and discovered the food programs.

No one dies on the food programs. No one is even ill. The worst thing that can happen is a chef sent home to sharpen his knives and return another day. The hosts of the demonstration shows are delighted to be cooking for you. A stream of chatter accompanies their moves from cutting board to oven to table. They note the tantalizing aromas. They are concerned with adding "a suggestion of heat." They identify "layers of flavor." Everything turns out just fine.

As I watched I began noticing things. The knives were not ruler shaped like the decades-old ones in my drawer but a sort of triangular, sail-like shape. Walking by a kitchen store, I found myself at the cutlery counter debating the merits of various models. To try out my purchase, I bought a. sack of vegetables of varying consistencies and made a minestrone. You can't walk around with a bowl of soup. I set the table, sat down, and ate.

The table was wrong. A rectangle in a square space can go either way. Switching it from vertical to horizontal, moving the chairs, and changing my place did not erase the pain of his empty seat but, strange to say, made it easier to bear.

I learned that you can't chew and cry at the same time. I learned that audiovisual aids help. A pot of bulbs in the center of the table—watching them grow day by day—helps. Listening to Bach helps. And sometimes nothing helps.

I tried some of the new recipes. Who knew you could make "smashed" potatoes without peeling those large Russets? That you could boil up small Yukon golds and mash with the skin on? And add spinach! That you didn't have to cook beets but could slice them very thin (with my new knife!), sprinkle with vinegar, and eat au natural? While I was at it, I might as well roast a chicken. Too much to eat myself. I invited someone over. There were tears as I arranged the store-bought cake on the plate; tears as I cleaned up later. But the meal itself was a success. Three hours passed like three hours.

Four years later the large pots and pans I used for our meals are stashed in the back of the cupboard for meals with guests. In the front are new, small, brightly colored pots and pans in which a single portion looks at home. I am back to creative cooking, putting together odd combinations of ingredients, dishes for one that sometimes delight and sometimes feed the garbage. But meals are good again.

I liked to garden at my home in Montauk but never bothered with indoor plants. They were just one more thing to take care of. Now the Montauk house and garden are gone—along with the strength for heavy lifting and agility for assuming uncomfortable postures—I reconsider. There are plants in various stages of bloom throughout the loft. I buy as they are just beginning to open. Each day they greet me with a new surprise.

Scott-Maxwell and Sarton are essentially homebound. I am not. Daily excursions to the outside world are a given in my life; longer times away are possible and frequently enjoyed. No matter how long I am gone, though, I must always return to mental and physical space that only I inhabit.

I find that the experience of having only myself to please is satisfying in ways I could not have imagined. In the beginning all I could do was long for the clutter and clatter of family life, the dinners for two centered about Roy's favorite foods, the sense of him always by my side through the long nights. I saw living alone as the cessation of small pleasures, just as I saw my inability to be as useful as before as a cessation to involvement in the big things that were an important role in my life.

Reading the authors, knowing that the changes of the present will accelerate in the future (less time outside with others, more time at home alone), I see that adjustments can be made, pleasure can be found. Using them as an example, I set my own course.

There are fewer professional meetings, and I take on less responsibility. Yet I find unanticipated fulfillment in the role of cheerleader to others. Sometimes just one suggestion will advance someone on a creative path I could never attain myself. Encouragement matters. And checks, however small, never hurt.

When I began reading May Sarton, I often grew impatient at her detailed descriptions of daily routine such as these:

> I am proud of the fact that I keep to such discipline as it took, for instance today with bad cramps, to get up and get my breakfast, carry it up on the tray, have it in bed, and then get up and make my bed and finally decide what to wear. That is always a problem because part of the discipline is to keep myself fed and keep the house more or less tidy on weekends when I

have no other help, and part of it is to try to look well, as well as I can. As I have said before, the routine is what keeps me from going to pieces. I might be crying, but if it is a little after four, as it is now, it is time to get up and go up to my desk and do something positive. About an hour later, it will be time to come down here, open my bed, and lay out my pajamas as if I had a servant to do that, lay out the book I am going to read, and the slippers that I am going to need for going down to get Pierrot in and put him out which happens over and over again during the night.

(1993:141–42)

Today I read her journal entries with new eyes. I remember my early years of making home visits to older clients in New York, half amused, half annoyed that everyone wanted me to come by at 1:00 in the afternoon. Didn't they know that I had to fit five interviews—scattered all over the city—into one day? *They* never went out. *They* seemingly had nothing to do. Why couldn't they be more flexible?

The need older people have for structure in their lives is all too clear to me now. It takes more time to prepare oneself and one's home for a guest— even (or especially) if it is a social worker, nurse, or physical therapist. In fact, it takes more time for everything.

Before Roy died, I never planned for the time between work and outside engagements. The time felt full. Finding myself alone facing a desert of time was terrifying. And more. With no one there to see me, it was easy to become invisible to myself. I realized how easy it would be to let myself fall into careless ways of self-care or housekeeping, to tell myself that it didn't matter because it was "only me." Forcing myself to the discipline of meals and sleep and exercise and work at regular times proved a salvation. It has not yet come to the point where I need a whole morning to prepare for a visitor, but I understand how an old person with limited strength might require that much time to put herself and her home in the best light. Where once I saw a rigidity, perhaps an excessive self-regard, I now see admirable qualities of grit and determination. What new insights are in store for me?

Many of my previous roles have gone. Others will follow. But the authors teach me that loss of roles in old age need not be a diminishment. Just the opposite. As I am forced to modify the principles of life as I knew it, I create opportunities to obtain them in new ways. My existence may no longer be validated by others, but I can continue to be real to myself.

9

JUST SHOW UP

Just show up. That's all we have to do, that's all I do when I am fully present,
for good or bad, right here, right now, without thinking about work or recess.
A sleeper can wake and be lured out of bed by the sorcery of the sky as day is
dawning. Time well spent. After all (or more accurately, during all), I may not
live to the end of this sentence, to lift my felt-tipped pen and settle a tiny black
dot on the page. I did. But that was then and this is now, the thisness of what
is, the ripening dawn.

—DIANE ACKERMAN, *DAWN LIGHT: DANCING WITH CRANES AND OTHER*
WAYS TO START THE DAY

JUST show up. Or, as the motto of the 1960s advised, be here now. The message is not new. Centuries-old teachings inform the Zen masters of today. Yoga, meditation, every popular movement of self-improvement urges us to be present in the moment. Easy to say. Hard to do.

As one who has tried and failed to achieve the goal of presence at various times throughout her life, I read Diane Ackerman's writing, and that of other authors who write of the experience, with dismay. It is not that I question the worthiness of the effort or the possibility of achieving it; rather, it seems to require a special gift enhanced by a superhuman effort.

Or perhaps only a nonurban existence. Can the gift of presence be acquired in late life by someone who has spent over half a century practicing the art of absence in a large city where many sights, sounds, and smells in the great surround are better ignored than noted? Riding the subway, waiting for buses, walking the streets, I have grown adept at detaching a large portion of my mind and senses from the scene—preserving just enough awareness to ensure safe arrival at my destination. When that destination happens to be a park, a performance, or a museum, it is easier. Savoring what lies before me is what I have come for. But even then, I am ashamed to say, my attention is often fragmented; it wanders off—a distracted toddler zigzagging along a path that leads farther and farther from the present moment.

Taking the writing of Ackerman—and the many other authors who have written so persuasively of the gifts of being present in the moment—as a challenge, I begin.

I invite the authors to walk with me through the city and begin to experience my surroundings through their eyes. I take pictures of things that catch my eye—an arrangement of vegetables at the greenmarket, children chasing squirrels in the park; I close my eyes and listen to the sounds around me, to differentiate among the odors in the air, to feel which way the wind is blowing.

At home I am more likely to give full attention to one activity at a time—eating without watching the news, listening to music without a book in hand. It doesn't always work, but every time it does, I am startled by the results. It is as if my senses had grown dull through disuse and I am polishing them, one by one.

As I return to the writing that inspires me to collect quotes for this chapter, I realize that none of the authors has discovered the idea of living mindfully in old age. It is an intrinsic part of who they are, who they have always been: keen observers, alert to the revealing sensual detail, noting and directing our attention to the fleeting nuances of daily life. So it is not that their works of youth or midlife lack examples of presence, it is the awareness that the day will soon come when showing up is no longer an option that makes individual moments of late life more precious, the necessity to capture them more compelling.

I also note the ways in which presence and loss are inextricably bound. The time ahead is not only limited in days, it is limited in what one can do within those days. Often suffering an assortment of physical woes, the authors celebrate what they can.

When Colette's age-related infirmities as well as the World War II German occupation of Paris keep her homebound, she writes:

> "Every evil of man arises from the fact that he is unable to stay quietly in his room." I quote approximately this phrase of Pascal, but without savouring it overmuch because I do not believe that wisdom consists of choosing immobility. But once immobilized, reduced to snapping up the most vivid and most assimilable of what happens within reach, I prefer to apply to our urban existence the phrase of a landowner jealous of his land: "Love what's on top, love what's beneath." Not that the "underneath" of the city has any charms, but, cut off from the exterior, let's enjoy what's within.
>
> (1975:153)

Colette moves from her limitations "once immobilized" to presence, "snapping up the most vivid and most assimilable of what happens within reach," to appreciation, "let's enjoy," to love, "'Love what's on top, love what's beneath." Once she makes the progression, I see it— in the quotes I have gathered, in moments from my own life when I first knew them to be true.

The power of appreciation in times of pain or incapacity appears in Florida Scott-Maxwell's journal: her personal account was the first book on aging I ever read. Reading Scott-Maxwell as a young social worker seeking insight into how it felt to be old, I noted how different she was from the clients I was seeing. Here was an old, disabled woman, living alone, who was not depressed, hopeless, lonely, or afraid. Here was a woman who did not mourn the past or complain about her physical losses. Here was a woman who found pleasure in daily life, however meager, and looked forward to the future.

She described her inner life in a compelling way. She was wise. I remembered the melody for years. Now I focus on the words.

This morning when I woke and knew that I had had a fair night, that my pains were not too bad, I lay waiting for the uplifting moment when I pull back the curtains, see the sky, and I surprised myself by saying out loud: "My dear, dear days."

(1968:39)

The enchantment of the sky, ever changing beauty, almost ignored. Beyond words, without form, not to be understood, or stated. It ravishes away dullness, worry, even pain. It graces life when nothing else does. It is the first marvel of the day. Even when leaden grey, it is still a friend, withdrawn for a time.

(77)

I pause over these quotes a long time. The desk where I write each morning faces a south window. Occasionally, as I pause to think about how best to phrase a thought, I glance up from the computer and am taken by surprise by a bright blue sky with fluffy white clouds. I note that the weather will be fair and suitable for whatever activities I have planned for later. And return to my work.

Today I make a conscious effort to pay attention—and see that the sky is dull, the "leaden gray" of a semi-industrial neighborhood in an urban area. I decide to look for five minutes and type what I see. Only then do I note that the sky is not one color at all, and surely not one consistency. Even with my flagging vision (how long will I see at all? I brush away the thought—concentrate!), I make out patterns and ridges, infinitesimal movement that reveals slivers of blue. Now and then, three or four birds—possibly seagulls though a bit smaller—fly east to west. River to river would be my guess.

I look down to type what I have seen; look up, and all has changed! The ridged mass of gray has almost dissolved; the wispiest of white cloud fragments in the lightest of blue have appeared. It is indeed, as Scott-Maxwell says, "a marvel!" And for her, it is only the first marvel of a day that follows a night that was just "fair," filled with pains that were "not too bad."

I recall some of the old people I visited in their homes: clients with stories of the endless nights, when pain and fear racked their sleep. No one ever mentioned the relief of the dawn, the sights and sounds that returned them to the comforting light of day. I did not think to ask about it, much less draw them to look with me out at the window, up at the sky, across at the apartments that faced theirs, below to the life of the street. We might have talked about what we saw; shared the experience of looking up and out from the problem before us to relish the experience of being alive in the world. It would have seemed loony, if not unprofessional, to do so. Still, I am struck by the potential.

M.F.K. Fisher feels that preparation for being old would help. If we anticipate the losses of old age, we will be better able to handle them. Appreciation of the moment—all the richer because of the deprivation from which it springs—is one of her recurring themes.

> What is important, though, is that our dispassionate acceptance of attrition be matched by a full use of everything that has happened in all the long wonderful, ghastly years to free a person's mind from his body . . . to use the experiences, both great and evil, so that physical annoyances are surmountable in an alert and even mirthful appreciation of life itself.
>
> Parts of the Aging Process are scary, of course, but the more we know about them, the less they need be. That is why I wish we were more deliberately taught, in early years, to prepare for this condition. It would leave a lot of us freed to enjoy the obvious rewards of being old, when the sound of a child's laugh, or the catch of sunlight on a flower petal is as poignant as ever was a girl's voice to an adolescent ear, or the tap of a golf-ball into its cup to a balding banker's.
>
> (1984:237)

What is most striking in the writing of Fisher and others is that presence is not cited as compensation for what has been lost—a late-life consolation prize. Attention to and appreciation of the moment is an achievement, in a class by itself. More than an achievement, it is, as Colette suggests, a form of love.

Alex Kates Shulman is in her seventies when she expands on this idea—writing of her experience as a caregiver after her husband sustains a fall that caused significant brain damage:

> When that tough-minded visionary philosopher Friedrich Nietzsche proposed his principle amor fati, love of fate—meaning "love your fate, which is in fact your life"—he wasn't suggesting that you love only the pleasant parts. He himself was suffering extreme physical pain at the time. No, to embrace life fully meant to him to accept life's inevitable limitations without hiding from them, no matter what fate had in store. "Amor fati," he said, is "not merely to endure necessity, still less to deny it, but to love it." Not a passive resignation, but an active embrace. He called it his "formula for greatness in a human being. "Amor fati!" Love your fate. Love what is. My fate took a turn on July 22, 2004. Absurd it would be to hide from it, or wish it away, much less to resist or rail against it as if it could be undone by an act of my puny will. Not enough even to merely accept it. To live life fully within my limitations I must struggle with it, adapt to it, make the best of it, milk it for all I can. Love it.
>
> (2008:165–66)

Loving what is—when your mind and heart are filled with love of what was—is the first lesson for a widow. I read a lot of Edith Wharton in the first months after Roy's death. There was something soothing about her fiction—a sense of order in the universe that counteracted my sense of rootlessness. But it was in the last paragraph of her autobiography—written when she was in her seventies, a few years before she died—that I came upon a line that was to become my mantra:

> Life is the saddest thing there is, next to death; yet there are always new countries to see, new books to read (and, I hope, to write), a thousand little daily wonders to marvel at and rejoice in, and those magical moments when the mere discovery that "the woodspurge has a cup of three" brings

not despair but delight. The visible world is a daily miracle for those who have eyes and ears; and I still warm my hands thankfully at the old fire, though every year it is fed with the dry wood of more old memories.

(1933:379)

"The woodspurge has a cup of three." A simple phrase; gorgeous and mysterious. But what in the world is a woodspurge? And where did the quote come from? Looking it up, I find it comes from a poem by Rosetti (which Wharton must have imagined that everyone of her day would recognize) describing a state of great despair, lifted by a chance observance in the garden. The woodspurge, as it turns out, is a plant that usually has two blooms (or cups), and this one had three! For weeks I quoted the line to myself at odd moments throughout the day—finding deep comfort in its sound and meaning.

Reading Wharton, among others, I note that it is not presence alone that brings pleasure, comfort, or love. It may be necessary to "just show up," but what we bring along with us makes a difference. Guests to the party of life, we cannot come empty-handed.

The ability to recall and quote appropriately from prior reading is a gift of many authors. Evocation of past authors enriches the present experience. After I note that Wharton quotes Rosetti without attribution, I recall that Colette paraphrases Pascal, Shulman cites Nietzsche, and then recall that May Sarton uses a phrase by Simone Weil in the second of her memoirs—a phrase to which she refers again in later volumes.

Simone Weil says, "Absolute attention is prayer." And the more I have thought about this over the years, the truer it is for me. If one looks long enough at almost anything, looks with absolute attention at a flower, a stone, the bark of a tree, grass, snow, a cloud, something like revelation takes place. Something is "given," and perhaps that something is always a reality *outside* the self. We are aware of God only when we cease to be aware of ourselves, not in the negative sense of denying the self, but in the sense of losing self in admiration and joy.

(1973:99)

Enrichment of the present by recalling apt citations is possible for women in full possession of their mental capacities—women long practiced in the power of language to enhance understanding and appreciation of life's simplest pleasures. But what help is there for those of us who have never acquired that frame of reference? Or who have lost whatever cognitive ability they once possessed?

I recall the delight that many older adults with dementia take in the moment—savoring sweet foods, staring in wonder at colored bubbles floating in the air, tapping feet to rhythms of song. Devoid of memory and often of words, they cannot let us in on what is going on within. Although it is good to have the ability to encase sensory details in words, to bring out and sort through like photographs when we feel the need. It is also good to know that the senses endure after the intellect fades.

Colette elicits not only past reading but past experiences to enhance her present moment. Reading her, I wonder if the sensory banquet she describes so fully is present in inchoate form in those who have lost the gift of expression but not some residual memory of pleasure.

> The fragrance of riverside reeds, of spearmint, of eddying, disturbed water mingling with the parlous and pervasive savour of caltrops, these delights are not yet destined to escape, not for this year at any rate, one who has the wits to keep them safe in her Paris room—by denomination a writer increasingly under the dominance of her malady, but each day afforded relief by the faithful memory of her brain and of her subtle senses that in old age have lost none of their cunning.
>
> (1963:57)

The notion of a diminished life being enriched by absolute attention to what remains is given a twist by Doris Grumbach, who wrote many books on her aging experience. Setting herself the challenge of chronicling every detail of her daily life, she finds that reduction of possibilities need not come from outer circumstances. It can come from within.

Eternity in an hour. I have become a minimalist of experience. Once I thought I could never travel to all the places I wanted to see, but in old age, the cove, in the variety of its seasons and weathers and times, seems to satisfy my need for new sights. . . . Yesterday afternoon, listening to music in the new room, I thought about how my musical taste has suffered a similar sea change. . . . Season after season . . . I went to hear *Der Ring des Nibelungen*, I wallowed (is that too denigratory a word?) in the vast, lush, overwrought score, the wordy, rich libretto, the larger-than-life, huge-voiced singers and the garish sets . . . then . . . I began to prefer symphonies and concerti, still on the opulent side of music, but without grand opera décor. In middle age, I found I had become fond of chamber music, and in the last few years, listening to a recording of Glenn Gould performing his extraordinary, second version of The Goldberg Variations, I realized that I have again switched my allegiance. Now I prefer the variety, the ample swell and sweet decline the abundant tones of a single instrument. *The world in a grain of sand.* Now there is no further retreat possible, except into that antithesis of music: silence. Like everyone else, of course, I will come to that.

(1996:11)

Grumbach does not point to any deficit in hearing or cognition that prompts her change in "allegiance" from grand opera to chamber music to solo instrument. It is simply an evolving preference. But something else is operating here—which is clearly stated in the last line. She is in "retreat" to a time that will inevitably lead to silence, or death. The realization does not impede appreciation of music in general (which seems as strong as ever).

A complement to Grumbach's views on music can be found in the last diary of Anaïs Nin. I had assumed that the multiple diaries of Nin—depicting her erotic adventures of 1930s Paris—had ceased as she grew older. By the time they were popularized by feminists of the 1970s, the accompanying picture of a woman in late middle age unconvincingly striking the pose of a younger self pointed in that direction. And yet she had continued—in her seventies and in the end stages of cancer—effectively adapting her gift for minute examination and description of the passing moment.

In music I feel most deeply the passing of things. A note strikes. It evokes an image. But with another note, this image is altered, it moves, it fades, it passes slowly, it melts into another image. Images of beauty and sorrow pass thus before me and are carried away in the forward movement of music. The note that was struck, and vanished, carried away with its sound the things that are precious. It left, with its echoes, an echo of things that are gone. Between it and the other note that is coming, there is a space that holds a loss and an emptiness. Music holds the movements of life, the chained incidents which compose it, the eternal melting of one note before another to create song. The notes must melt before one another; they must be lost after they have given their soul, for the sake of the whole. It may be a beautiful note, but it cannot strike alone forever. It must pass, as all things must pass, to make up the immense composition that is life.

(1980:181)

Grumbach writes: "the antithesis of music: silence. Like everyone else, of course, I will come to that." Nin writes: "It must pass, as all things must pass." Their relationship to music is their relationship to life. And the sense of an ending adds to their appreciation. It is an important lesson but one I need less than others. In fact it is *only* in listening to music that I have ever experienced the gift of presence spoken of by many authors. As I grow old, I crave music, in its infinite variety, more and more. My challenge lies elsewhere.

Seeking an experience of rapt attention, I take to the park without book, phone, computer, pen, or pad. I will sit on a bench for an hour and simply be. It takes time for my mind to remove itself from its concerns and settle down. It takes more time to silence questions and judgments about the passing scene: What language is that couple speaking? Doesn't that man know you're not supposed to smoke in the park? Finally my attention falls on a baby of six or seven months in a carriage a few feet away while her nanny chats on a cell phone.

This is one busy baby—having just discovered what she can do with her hands and feet. She turns them individually at first: this way and that. Then she gets them all waving together. Her face registers amazement. She cries out in delight.

Watching her, I am stabbed with regret. I was a young, impatient mother. Oblivious to the wonders around me, waiting for the day I could try my wings in the wider world, I did not know the time I was living through would be so short, the time ahead so long.

I console myself, walking home: that was then, this is now. I am still alive, still present. There are still moments to show up for. And remember to call an old friend whom I last saw at her husband's funeral two weeks ago. She cried when anyone mentioned his death, a moment after which she joyfully greeted everyone, a moment after which she asked why he hadn't yet arrived. My friend suffers from multi-infarct dementia, which completely robbed her of short-term memory while leaving her personality intact. She is the most sociable person I have ever known. The two great parties she gave each year—Labor Day and New Year's Eve—were only punctuation marks in a life filled with activities and people she loved who loved her.

My friend is delighted to hear my name, my voice. In that instant of remembering, she asks after Roy and I tell her (as I have for the past four years) that, sadly, he has died. And she tells me (as she has for the past four years) how she always liked him, what a fine man he was. We agree on that. And are back again on how good it is to hear from me, how much she appreciates the call, how we should talk soon again. Then she says, as she always does, "I thought you had forgotten all about me." And I say, as I always do, "I could never forget you." We hang up in a flurry of good wishes. I picture her lapsing back into her chair, lonely, feeling abandoned. I know that if I call back in five minutes we will repeat the same routine. It was only a passing moment. But we both were there.

10

FIERCE WITH REALITY

You need only claim the events of your life to make yourself yours. When you truly possess all you have been and done, which may take some time, you are fierce with reality. When at last age has assembled you together, will it not be easy to let it all go, lived, balanced, over?

—FLORIDA SCOTT-MAXWELL, *THE MEASURE OF MY DAYS*

THIS book is my effort at self-assemblage. And indeed it takes some time. I remember opening the large box that arrived from IKEA holding the shelves, brackets, and screws that were to constitute a new bookcase. How could there possibly be so many pieces for such a simple, solid structure? The instruction book was written in three languages and even had a pictorial representation. I laughed at the opening line: all that was needed to complete the job was "a screwdriver and a friend." That one was easy enough to solve—I provided the screwdriver and coffee while not one but two friends (or, more accurately, a son and *his* friend) took over.

I would like to take Scott-Maxwell literally, to believe that the passing years will magically fit all my pieces together while I sit sipping coffee and looking on. But I doubt that is what she meant at all. It will take some effort on my part. There will be no instruction book. And I must find a language of my own.

Scott-Maxwell's language is an interesting place to start; her observation ends not with a period but a question mark. Whether possession and acceptance of all I have been and done will result in ease in letting it all go is far from certain. There are at least two authors whose last words and days argue against her premise.

I think first of Carolyn Heilbrun, the noted professor, writer, critic, and mentor to a generation of feminist scholars, According to all reports, her suicide at age seventy-seven had no known precipitant. She was married with three grown children and a still active career. There were no known health problems; in fact she had taken a long walk just that morning with a colleague who had not perceived anything amiss.

The popular press echoed literary journals in wondering at her reasons and mourning her loss. As I returned to her books for this project, I found that the reason—like Poe's purloined letter—was hidden in plain sight. The genesis and development of the idea evolved over time.

In *Writing a Woman's Life* when she was sixty-four and considering the idea of old age for herself, she wrote:

> I do not believe that death should be allowed to find us seated comfortably in our tenured positions. Instead, we should make use of our security, our seniority, to take risks, to make noise, to be courageous, to become unpopular. . . . Neither rocking on a porch; nor automatically offering her services as cook and housekeeper and child watcher, nor awaiting another chapter in the heterosexual plot, the older woman must be glimpsed through all her disguises which seem to preclude her right to be called woman. She may well for the first time be woman herself.
>
> (1989:131)

These positive words echo Scott-Maxwell's idea of an old woman finally claiming her own identity.

Yet a year later, writing of the suicide of Virginia Woolf, Heilbrun observes:

> She chose to end her life before the chance to make the decision for herself could be taken from her. Having totted up the score, she decided that death was the way for her. True she said in her last note to Leonard that she feared

madness again. There had been madness in her past, but madness now was, I suspect, not the heart of the matter; it was simply the easiest way to describe despair, or the clear decision that life in her sixties, given the conditions of her world, was simply not worth the terrible effort it would have cost.

(1990:93)

Life seems to brighten for Heilbrun as she retires from her academic position and takes on new projects. Hopefulness is present even in the title of her book *The Last Gift of Time*. Yet reading the introduction in the light of what we know of her future is chilling.

I had long held a determination to commit suicide at seventy. Yet for a time the fact that my sixties had offered such satisfaction only confirmed my life-long resolution not to live past "threescore years and ten." Quit while you're ahead was, and is, my motto. . . . True my life was good. But is it not better to leave at the height of well-being rather than contemplate the inevitable decline and the burden one becomes upon others. . . . I find it powerfully reassuring now to think of life as "borrowed time." Each day one can say to oneself: I can always die; do I choose death or life? I daily choose life the more earnestly because it is a choice.

(1998:7)

It could be argued that Heilbrun's suicide was not contrary to Scott-Maxwell's premise but a confirmation of it: choosing when and how to die rather than leaving the time and circumstances up to fate was proof that her act of assemblage was complete. A second look, however, reveals an inconsistency. She did not wish to decline and have her life become a burden to others and yet did not imagine that her suicide could pose an even greater burden—of sorrow, guilt, and never-ending questioning—to those she left behind.

Then I turn to Marguerite Duras. She clung to life and fought death with all her might—long after everyone else had given up hope for her, long after she was bedbound, in need of total care, and could only gasp out words of protest.

The title of her book *C'est Tout* becomes, in the English translation, *No More*. In it we see her transcribed deathbed utterances to Yann, who she saw as the great love of her life. The very recording of the words and the accompanying literary analysis (that occupies more of the text than her words themselves) are testimony to Duras's importance to a segment of the French intelligentsia at the time of her death. The dated transcriptions are sometimes incoherent, often filled with yearning for Yann, and throughout filled with anguish and rage.

DECEMBER 8

You are all a bunch of idiots.
You're completely fucked up.
It's all unbearable.

JANUARY 3

All I know is that I have nothing left.
That is the horror. Nothing left but the
void. The voids. This void of the last
terrain.
There are not two of us. Each of us is alone.

FEBRUARY 19

I know that I am going to undergo death,
What awaits me: my face in the morgue.
What a horror, I don't want that.

FEBRUARY 28

It's over.
All over.
It is the horror.

As the translator, Richard Howard, prefaces the volume: "Here is nothing but what the French call hargne (surliness, resentment, bad temper), tense and often mocking observances of the still articulate soul, betrayed by the still-longing body" (1995:10–11).

It would seem that the deaths of Heilbrun and Duras could not be more different. One actively seeks death. The other fights it with her last breath. Yet they are both examples of the extremes to which the need to be in control of one's death can lead.

I could interpret them both as cautionary tales of life endings I do not wish to emulate and move on to more positive examples. Yet something holds me here: the idea that assembling the pieces of oneself may be essential but not be enough.

Although the theory and practice of life review had originated earlier (Butler 1963), it was not until the early 1980s that reminiscence became an accepted part of gerontological practice. It was no surprise to practitioners that old people liked to talk about the past. In fact, an enduring stereotype of the aged had long been their propensity to dwell on "the old days."

What was new was the idea that helping older people revisit their earlier selves was a therapeutic intervention; that revisiting the past was a way to come to terms with all one had been and done before the days of being and doing were over.

As a social work practitioner and teacher, I was wholeheartedly committed to this development. Like many of my colleagues, I marveled at the stories and rejoiced as clients reclaimed lost parts of themselves and came to see their experiences as a legacy to those who would come after. Some clients were helped to record their stories to pass on to grandchildren or to be placed in an archive.

So compelling was the act of helping older people assemble pieces of their past lives that we often had to remind ourselves that we were not oral historians whose task ended with the collection of stories but social workers charged with helping our clients meet the challenges of the present and discuss their hopes and fears for the future.

Now, as old as many of my clients were then, I find it far easier to face the knowns of my past than the unknowns of my future. And it is how I prepare to meet that future that interests me most. I may have to give up control of my life at the end. But, until I arrive there, choices remain within my power.

I find myself turning most often to M.F.K. Fisher and Doris Grumbach, both of whom chose to meet the infirmities of age with a realistic blend of acceptance and hope.

Fisher is already feeling multiple effects of Parkinson's disease when she writes in *Sister Age* (1984:235): "I notice that as I get rid of the protective covering of the middle years, I am more openly amused and incautious and less careful socially, and that all this makes for increasingly pleasant contacts with the world."

In an interview about her thoughts on aging, she states: "I would really like, in my last years—which I know these to be—to leave an impression of a mild enjoyment and tolerance and courtesy. . . . I'd like to be rather graceful about my last years" (1992:96).

By the time she writes *Last House* (1995), her physical situation has deteriorated to the point where she cannot write on her own. Here is her response to a letter from an old friend complaining about upcoming surgery. She begins with a lecture about how he must accept all this as a part of aging and concludes:

> I look out the window and the leaves are getting dancier than ever and suddenly I feel like shooting my wheelchair across the tiles, and then your letter floats onto the tile floor and I can't even pick it up and I start to titter and so does my helpless friend who is typing for me, and altogether I feel quite silly and giddy and happy, and I am not at all peeved at you, poor man.
>
> (278)

Fisher seems to have an innate propensity toward good cheer. We see her finding joy in the moment through her food and travel writing as well as in her memoirs. It permeates all her writing from the beginning to the end of life. This is not the case with Doris Grumbach, who began with a less sanguine view of the human condition.

Grumbach lamented the aging process as she approached her seventieth birthday. *Coming into the End Zone* (1991) is a book that dwells on loss—of her own physical powers and the AIDS-related ends of friends and colleagues. Yet by the time she reaches eighty, her view has tempered. As realistic as ever about what she is facing and might face in the future, she chooses to mark the milestone birthday at a party with family and friends.

> Old age is both the final limitation and the ultimate prison. From it there is no chance for escape or improvement. It is beyond pardon or commutation, it is the period to the sentence of change. Nonetheless, I have decided to have a celebration, as if these dire bounds did not exist, as if hope of some small future was still a thing with feathers.
>
> (2000:14)

"Nonetheless!" I embrace that word as summing up all that will characterize my days from now until my death. Here my imagination comes to a halt. How am I to think about, prepare for this inevitable event?

I turn first to Marilyn French who experienced a decade living with the effects of esophageal cancer and its treatments before her death.

> When we die, all we are possessed of is our experience. It is one part of our lives that is largely in our own control. We have no control over where we are born, our sex, color, or size, our intelligence and talents: we have only limited ability to change our class or economic status; and no control at all over the twists of history, which with utter caprice and randomness can toss us into a death camp, a peaceful quiet period, an economic depression, or an exciting period of renaissance. Most of us spend much of our lives simply coming to terms with the inexorable conditions of our lives. But we ourselves choose the way we take, deal with, think and feel about, and respond to those conditions. This area of life, the experiential, is most completely ours; it is what defines us and the quality of our lives. It—not

accomplishment, wealth, worldly power, or fame—is the only real measure of a life. And only we ourselves can assign our lives a "grade." The richer, deeper, and more varied our thoughts and feelings, the wider and richer our interactions and connections, the richer our life. When we are old and look back, it is only this that matters. The rest is all props.

(1998:245–46)

Next I consider Diana Athill who, at age eighty-five, extends the idea of what matters at the time of death to fear of the event itself:

The big event of old age—the thing which replaces love and creativity as a source of drama—is death. Probably the knowledge that it can't fail to come fairly soon is seriously frightening. I say "probably" because to be as frightened as I suspect I might be would be so disagreeable that I have to dodge it—as everyone must, no doubt. There are many ways of dodging. The one I favor is being rational, saying "Everyone who ever was, is and shall be, comes to the end of life. So does every *thing*. It is one of the absolute certainties, as *ordinary* as anything can be, so it can't be all that bad." Having said that, you then allow your mind to occupy itself with other matters—you do not need to force it, it is only too pleased to do so.

(2002:5–6)

She returns to the theme several years later:

My own belief—that we on our short-lived planet are part of a universe, simultaneously perfectly ordinary in that *there it is* and incalculably mysterious in that it is beyond our comprehension—does not feel like believing in nothing and would never make me recruit anyone for slaughter. It feels like a state of infinite possibility, stimulating and enjoyable—not exactly comforting, but acceptable because true.

(2008:43)

Athill could have stopped with that, but she does not. She goes on to think of what will survive her:

If, flitting in and out of our awareness, there are people who are *beginning*, to whom the years ahead are long and full of who knows what, it is a reminder—indeed it enables us to feel again—that we are not just dots at the end of thin black lines projecting into nothingness, but are parts of the broad many-coloured river teeming with beginnings, ripenings, decayings, new beginnings—are still parts of it, and our dying will be part of it just as these children's being young is, so while we still have the equipment to see this, let us not waste our time grizzling.

(84)

I am comforted to think of myself as part of that "broad many-coloured river" of life at the time of my death. To worry less about the individual legacy I leave to those who know me and to think more about all those who I will never know.

Alice Walker helps me imaginatively enter that state.

In deep meditation the self, the ego busy with its many projects, completely disappears. It is the most delightful experience imaginable. Perhaps death will be like this. You are sitting there, but light is streaming right through the place where you sit. This experience can be had in motion, too, and is the experience we have when giving ourselves away. It is as if we are dissolving into everything and everyone around us and we recognize the illusion of separateness. And when someone thanks you for something, you thank *them* because you realize it is only their acceptance of their gift that allows you to give.

Sit with the thought of erasing yourself so that others might more gracefully arrive. One easy way to do this is to imagine the spot you are sitting in without you. It will remain full of itself, which contains also, somehow, the invisible essence of you.

(2006:45–46)

The quotations throughout this book— and my meditation on their personal relevance—prove Walker's point. Through the words of others I have come to my own words. The work of assembling myself is an ongoing project that shares space with other projects where the authors have provided guidance: how to live the days until my death and how to think about the world after I leave it.

Many of the authors I cite most frequently have now left the world, but the space they occupied is, as Walker suggests, filled with their essence.

Doris Grumbach, who felt herself old at seventy, decided on hope at eighty, is now alive and writing over the age of ninety. It seems fitting to let her words be the last words.

At the moment my contemporaries and I are on "holding ground," the maritime term for a place to anchor temporarily for the night. This haven will not serve for very long, the way childhood had seemed to and youth and maturity did. Old age is terminal, but still, I find the long habit of living hard to break.

The fortunate among us will die quickly. James F. Fries termed it "compressed vitality." But there will be the exceptions who will disintegrate slowly. A hip, a knee, a vital organ, one part at a time, unlike the old conveyance in Oliver Wendell Holmes's one-horse shay in "The Deacon's Masterpiece." That old carriage had served without a part failing or needing replacement for a century. Then, when it was 100 years old, it collapsed, fell down, and died, all at once.

However death arrives, in installments or in one instant stroke, I regard myself as fortunate. I will be able to echo the last words of Lady Mary Wortley Montague (who died in 1762):

"It has all been very interesting."

(2011)

I say, Amen.

CONCLUSION

Aging, I Write

Anyone is made different by the work into which he pours his energies.
The more of himself he gives to it, the more his vocation shapes him to its
purposes. The practice of an art through which the whole person translates
what he receives from life into terms which others can understand, feel,
and enjoy shapes a person most of all.
—BERTHA CAPEN REYNOLDS, *LEARNING AND TEACHING*
IN THE PRACTICE OF SOCIAL WORK

T HE front cover of Reynolds's book features a teacher standing in front
of a huge blackboard on which large cursive writing is barely visible.
She is holding a long pole with a pointed tip which, we can assume, will
not be used to poke recalcitrant students but to call attention to this word
or that. Her hairdo and dress, as those of the women who face her, mark
them of a different time. The text, first published in 1942, was based on
Reynolds's work during the Great Depression.

Over seventy years have passed, along with thousands of books on
social work. I have yet to find one that so fully captures the sense of how
practice of our profession (as any work to which one gives oneself fully)
changes us.

I particularly like Reynolds's view that the very act of teaching "shapes a person most of all." It is akin to the three sayings that I used to post on the board at the beginning of every class on supervision:

To teach is to learn twice.
If you're not learning, you're not teaching.
We teach what we need to learn.

I began this book with "Aging, I Wrote"—a review of all that I thought and taught before entering that stage of life myself. I ended that chapter with an image of the authors as sherpas, using their hard-won knowledge of the landscape to guide me on my way.

I end this book teaching what I still need to learn.

Authors as sherpas. Authors as lionesses. It is as hard to fix on one metaphor as it is to fix on one lesson. How to identify the myriad effects of mind on mind? I am, after all, one reader, making connections to one life. So I hesitate to draw far-reaching conclusions.

And yet, as I reflect on what I have learned from my reading and my own experience as an old woman, I cannot resist one more opportunity to be a teacher. Using Reynolds's notion of translation (without the didactic pointer that her publisher chose to put on the cover), I ask myself one question: what do I know now that I didn't know then?

I knew about the losses of self and others endemic to the aging process. I did not know their fluctuating effect on one's state of mind. Bad days come without advance notice and tend to hang around a while. Good days are equally unpredictable.

I knew that in the face of diminished capacity one had to slow down. I did not know that—in a process as mysterious as the ebb and flow of hope—one's desires keep pace with one's possibilities. And that the lessening of big adventures increases the joy of small ones. How much else remains to be revealed to me?

Last, and perhaps most important: helper and helped have an equal stake in the outcome of their encounter.

Practitioner and client are both vulnerable (that is to say, mortal), both living in time. For the old person, it is the existential issue of time running out. For the practitioner, it is the practical issue of increasing caseloads: less time for each client, less time to seek, listen, and respond to all that falls between the lines on the ubiquitous form that links needs to services.

I think of Joan Didion, who writes, "When we lose that sense of the possible we lose it fast" (2011:183).

Losing that sense of the possible. Whether it is lost fast or slowly (and it would seem to vary), it plagues old people and practitioners alike. No time for everything soon becomes no time for anything. I do not rush to pin the label of "clinical depression" on the old person or "compassion fatigue" on the worker. It seems something larger. The loss of a sense of the possible, the loss of hope in the face of time's inexorable march.

I think way back to my earliest clients—the exceptions who retained a sense of purpose, identity, and continuity in old age: the majority who saw life as a mere succession of assaults.

On bad days I think of myself as one of the latter, as the fictional character in the short story "By and By," to whom Amy Bloom gives the words, "I miss every piece of my dead. Every piece is stacked high like cordwood within me, and my heart, both sides, and all four parts, is their reliquary" (2010:178). And as I carry that reliquary around on increasingly unsteady legs, I am tempted to despair. Then I think back to Pollyanna.

Remember Pollyanna? She was the eponymous heroine of a children's classic written over a century ago and popular when I was growing up in the 1940s. All I remembered was her preternatural cheeriness, the ability to find something to be "glad" about in the worst of situations. Then I went back to read the book and was surprised to find that she was not innately disposed toward happiness. As an orphan cast on the mercy of unwelcoming relatives, it certainly did not arise from her life situation. She was taught the "Glad Game" by her father before his death. Being glad was a learned skill—what we today might call a "coping mechanism." And it wasn't learned once and for all. Playing the Glad Game was a decision Pollyanna made with each new setback in her life. Unable to control what happened to her, she learned to control how she responded.

When Pollyanna hoped to find a doll in the charity package and got a pair of crutches, she could be glad that she didn't need them. When she lost the power of her legs and needed crutches, she could be glad of all the people who visited and told her how much her sunny outlook had meant to them. By the end of the book, Pollyanna has recovered the ability to walk and goes on to teach others to play the Glad Game.

Improbable, sentimental, and moralistic as the story reads, it is impossible not to see its message in most of the quotes of old women cited throughout this book. With a new twist. Pollyanna's resumption of previous functioning—a validation of her positive view of life—is not an option in old age. What is lost is lost forever. What little is gained can never take its place.

Then I think of the authors whose words fill these pages—all but a few of them could be seen as aging Pollyannas. They aren't glad because the bad events of their lives remind them of how fortunate they are. They recognize the impossibility of restitution. They will never again be who they were. Yet they retain a sense of the possible because they choose to do so.

A sentence or paragraph from one of their writings was enough to set me off on an inward quest. As I read, I realized how much was possible in a diminished life if one held on to that sense of self, placing the "the possible" in several dimensions of time.

As I wrote, I discovered what of my past was alive in my present and the meaning that could hold for my future.

The authors helped me see the possible in the past, where old people are prone to dwell. Their writing shows that when they settle in and stay for a while, it is with a purpose. Happy recollections of past pleasures as well as a laying to rest of past regrets (easier said than done!) are good reasons. Lamenting time wasted and opportunities missed are not.

The possible is in the present, where each day offers them opportunity for a small pleasure or a great insight; the day, as Diane Ackerman reminds us, begins before many of us are awake to witness it. It begins with the dawn. It is not for nothing that *dawn* and *a new day* have entered our lexicon as metaphors for hope. It is important to believe that good things can still happen for us. We old women may not be visible to anyone but ourselves, but we can be glad of the opportunity for us to become our own "new, improved products" until the moment of our deaths.

The possible is the future, only a sliver of which we will live to see. The future is so vast and so long! We will occupy little of it; still there is world enough and time to dig more deeply into the well of self and let its contents flow into the world. Alice Walker suggests we picture the space we are now occupying after we are gone. I do so and am gladdened to see many signs that my life, like every life that is or was, matters.

And I think of my own recent experience as a client, of being the bent figure greeting an unknown helper at the door. I remember it took but a moment for a caring presence to make itself known. Acceptance, respect, curiosity about who I was, what I hoped and feared took a few minutes more of close listening and observation. This helper had no time to probe for my backstory. As we spoke of what I could no longer do, he observed and commented on what remained to me. Then he suggested a few things I might try and was off to see the others on his long list.

Because I knew that I had the freedom to choose how I responded to the pelvic fractures that had rendered me suddenly walker-bound, he became a catalyst for what was already inside me. But many old people, alone with their own grim thoughts, have much that is dormant within them. Many could find a ray of possibility in even limited doses of that kind of attention. We cannot claim that less is more—in the practitioner's work or in the old person's life. But less is better than none. That alone can be cause for celebration.

Practitioners can be glad that each workday holds an opportunity to offer help and support to someone who needs it—and find comfort in the realization that a small intervention (a word here, a referral there) can have large, beneficial consequences. They can be grateful that work with the aged provides a crash course in philosophy, religion, psychology, sociology, biology, anthropology, history, and geography. All life's phases, all its sorrows and joys, are found there, as well as a range of ways to respond to them.

Those who work with the aged can be glad that they are helping themselves as they are helping the old people in their care. Shaping their own identities, they see models of who they do and do not wish to become. There is no better equipment for living.

Bertha Reynolds was one of the first social work theorists to move from "case to cause" to link private troubles with public issues. Unlike the Depression, which could be traced to economic conditions, aging is the human condition—and many of the issues related to it will always be personal. Still, they have public consequences, pubic ramifications, and require public responses.

And yet the words of the individual writer and their reverberations within the individual reader continue to be necessary. They do not need to be scrawled on a blackboard or underscored by a pointer to make their mark.

AFTERWORD

Bright as Stars in the Heaven of My Mind

Yes, it is a din of voices that I hear; and they do not all say the same thing. But the fit of thoughtfulness unites them. . . . Forbears, models, spirits whose influence and teachings I am now inseparable from, and forever grateful for. I go nowhere, I arrive nowhere, without them. With them I live my life, with them I enter the event. I mold the meditation, I keep if I can some essence of the hour, even as it slips away. And I do not accomplish this alert and loving confrontation by myself and alone, but through terrifying and continual effort, and with this innumerable, fortifying company, bright as stars in the heaven of my mind.

—MARY OLIVER, *WINTER HOURS*

MARY Oliver identifies her "great" ones: "Shelley and Fabre, and Wordsworth—the young Wordsworth—and Barbara Ward, and Blake, and Basho, Maeterlink and Jastrow, and sweetest Emerson, and Carson, and Aldo Leopold" (1999:20).

Oliver's greats are not mine (I don't even recognize most of their names), yet her sentiment rings true. I particularly like the way she speaks of them as "the young Wordsworth" and "the sweetest Emerson." The stars in her heaven are not a cluster; each is seen by and for itself; each casts its own glow.

This book is my personal star map, limning the ways in which the authors have spoken to me. Now I wish to speak directly to them—and by extension provide a more expansive introduction to those who have met them through glancing descriptions in these pages.

For a long time, I sought to accomplish my aim through a verbal version of Judy Chicago's iconic installation *The Dinner Party*. A feminist statement of the 1970s, the massive structure retains its original power. Thirty-nine plates—each representing a woman of distinction—are arranged historically and shaped in a triangle, as is the table on which they appear. Each plate contains an emblem, a representation of their contribution to the advancement of women. There is no conversation among the plates, though the vaginal layout shouts its own message.

Then it struck me that there was something inherently wrong about the impression that each individual had the same impact on me. Although in truth I didn't actually *know* these women any more than Judy Chicago knew hers, it felt as if I did. In fact, over the years of my reading, I had developed a group of what kids today call BFFs (best friends forever).

From childhood on, whatever our circumstances, we choose people we want as our friends; whether or not they necessarily want to "friend" us (in Facebook parlance) is another matter entirely. The "imaginary friend" to whom I confided my early troubles had the warmth and appreciation of one of my grandmothers—only my age and pretty, with the round frame, straight blond hair, and blue eyes much admired in the Boston of my day and entirely the opposite of all I was.

Looking over the company I wish to keep today, I congratulate myself on developing judgment and taste with the years. My BFFs are not necessarily the authors I quoted the most. A few appear on these pages again and again. Others are cited only once. It was the effect of their observations on me, the degree to which they inspired me to take some of their qualities within myself, that inspired me to single some out for special mention.

Their writing—fictional, polemic, poetic—forms the background music of my days. Maybe I missed some of the writing that the authors would wish to represent them. Some were considered but ultimately did not fit the book's structure. Others that would have been appropriate probably escaped my attention. My loss, surely. Sometimes I cite many of their publications and select just one quote. Other times I consult one book and quote from it repeatedly. The choices are idiosyncratic and so not defensible by any rationale but my own need to learn how to face old age with courage and grace.

As my mind's eye pulls up the image of each of my cherished authors, I speak to them in turn.

MAYA ANGELOU (1928–2014)

Each poem, each story, each essay you write contains a lesson. It should be irritating. It should be infuriating, to be lectured to. But it isn't. Even if we have not literally heard your melodious amber honey voice, its cadences seduce the eye as well as the ear. I see you as more of a teacher than a preacher; the sort of teacher who intuits the hidden potential of her students and can walk the tightrope between support and constructive criticism to help them see it in themselves.

You lived many lives before settling down to the writing for which you are known. An African American woman brought up by a grandmother in the South at the time of Jim Crow, a woman who reunited with parents in California when fully grown, a woman who endured childhood rape and embraced early motherhood; your many memoirs reflect the fullness of your life and the lessons it held for you.

Your particular gift in teaching is telling stories of your own experiences of failure, of embarrassment, of shame. You see yourself as many readers see themselves—a woman who makes mistakes, recognizes and apologies for them, and goes on to make them again and again. How can you not forgive yourself or we not forgive you when your situation rings so true!

DIANA ATHILL (1917–)

To think I might never have heard of you, had I not come upon your work by accident on a library shelf! To think that, born in 1917, you continue to live and write as lucidly and sensibly as ever well into your nineties! You are something of a lately discovered national treasure in England— a distinguished but not generally known editor of other people's writing

(V. S. Naipaul and Philip Roth) until getting down to your own memoirs after retirement. You come from long-lived British stock, and your early days sound a lot like those we see on *Downton Abbey*, the BBC import popular in the United States these past few years. American fans of English literature know that unconventional adults often emerge from such conventional childhoods.

You were no exception. You said "no" to having children at a time when you were expected to say "yes." You said "yes" to love with a black man at a time when you were expected to say "no." In your later years, you were very tied to your home, filled as it was with the books and objects of a lifetime; but I recently read that when you could no longer handle it, you moved into one room in an adult living facility and made a comfortable life there.

For all your writerly qualities, it is the ability to say the complex simply that I most admire. I return again and again to your wisdom about what it is to look death in the eye without flinching.

COLETTE (1873–1954)

Pick up any book of yours, turn to any page, and find a sensibility and a language that could not be mistaken for that of anyone else. The first sip of real milk after the end of the war, the way the light plays on water. Every blade of grass seemed to speak to you. Nothing was below your attention; yet you never got sucked up or in by experience. Just carried on.

You were born a good time before the other authors and lived through a significant part of the nineteenth and twentieth centuries before dying in Paris, in 1954 at age eighty-one. You came to Paris as a country girl, your hair so long you could sit on it. (How I love that detail.) Your husband exploited your writing, but you broke free and had a life of your own. You danced in the theater. You had your own line of cosmetics. You had male and female lovers—some much older, some much younger than yourself. You wrote fiction and nonfiction with equal ease. *Cheri* was based on a past event of your life, the heroine Lea, your age (fifty) at the time, looks back and says: "I love my past. I love my present. I'm not ashamed of what I've had, and I'm not sad because I have it no longer." You created your own epitaph—thirty years in advance.

Your last word was said to be "*regarde*" (look). It was in response to photographs before you but just as easily could be the motto of your life. You are in your apartment at the Palais Royale in Paris, in constant pain, writing on a lap desk by the light of your "blue lantern" (the pale blue writing paper you favored shading an ordinary bulb). Having your bed pushed out on the balcony so you could sleep "outdoors." You were sui generis. Each generation of women since your birth has discovered you anew. *Regarde*!

M.F.K. FISHER (1908–1992)

The poet W. H. Auden reportedly said of you, "I do not know of anyone in the United States today who writes better prose." You virtually invented the genre of food writing as literary art. Your trajectory is reminiscent of that of Julia Child. Growing up in California, raised on the sensible cuisine of your time and place, you felt your taste buds awakened on your first visit to France. That first meal in Dijon was to change your life and that of two generations of those who sought to describe food, review restaurants, and instruct the public on preparation and appreciation of the dining experience.

When you came on the scene, food writing focused on the ingredients of a dish and its preparation. None before you noted the obvious: that food is nourishment for the soul as well as the body; that food is the simplest and most profound of pleasures. I could say your unique innovation was putting yourself in the food story; creating a world around a meal; what you were thinking and feeling as well as tasting. Then I remember your language: elegant, learned, gorgeous.

All your non-food-related writing is noteworthy, but none more than *Last House*, a compilation of your late-life writing that was issued after your death. At the end you were eighty-three: crippled, unable to write, hardly able to speak. Still you were able to find simple sources of pleasure in your days. Under almost unthinkable obstacles, you sent us word of life in extremis, an object lesson in sheer will wedded to grace.

MARILYN FRENCH (1929–2009)

I am not in the habit of going to memorial services of people I don't know, but I went to yours. There were familiar faces—leaders in the feminist movement of the 1960s and 1970s on the stage and in the audience. There was a video running of your life; scenes of family life intermingled with social action. You had a gift for friendship. One after another, the women who were with you, from your political days through the ten-year battle with cancer that led to your death, painted a vibrant word portrait of you.

I remembered my early reading of *The Women's Room* and thinking, "Here is Lessing's *Golden Notebook* written about a midcentury American woman, a woman like me." There were other novels and articles through the years, but none moved me as much as *A Season in Hell*, in which you portrayed the consequences of choosing the most aggressive cancer treatments. As is often the case, you found effects of the treatment were more agonizing than the disease. At one point you were brought back from death and then berated everyone for not letting you go. Living on to suffer all the indignities of a diminished self, you came to an evaluation of your own life and a measurement by which others can evaluate theirs. (I have quoted it in "Fierce with Reality" and taken it as my mantra.)

DORIS GRUMBACH (1918–)

You felt old, you felt that your life was nearing the end as you approached age seventy—and continued writing of your aging experience all through your eighties. Although you had written some well-received fiction in your younger days, your greatest recognition was as cultural critic and essayist. You married young, had four children, and then in midlife began the intimate relationship with a woman that continues to your last days.

Yours was not a pleasant outlook on life or on impending death. You put your finger directly on the hard places of my defenses and pressed until it hurt. You wrote achingly about the untimely deaths of colleagues and friends to AIDS, of the many ways in which your body failed you.

Reading you was tough going. Still I returned to your writing again and again. I liked what you had to say about nature, about solitude, about the solace provided by the home on the cove in Maine that you and Sybil moved to in your late years. I pictured you as finally finding contentment there. So it was with great surprise that I came upon your last essay— written at the age of ninety—in *American Scholar*. You and Sybil had given up your home and moved together to an assisted living facility in Pennsylvania. Not only your residence but the tone of your writing has changed. You seem to have mellowed without losing any of your intellectual rigor and verbal acuity.

MADELEINE L'ENGLE (1918–2007)

You have a rare ability to weave many—often contradictory—pieces of your life into a coherent whole. Some elements you share with many women; balancing the calls of family and work, the inner and the outer life. Others arise at the point where science and religion meet. The works that I have quoted do not include the ones for which you are most famed; speculating on the wonders of time and space in a poetic style uniquely your own. What I have cited shows how you have infused all you know of the workings of the world we know with what you believe to be the world to come.

I picture you stealing away from the din of daily life to write your Crosswicks Journals. They are not the musings of the woman long removed from the hubbub of family and literary life for whom solitude provides ample space and time for reflection. Your writing is infused with a sense of necessity. Your inner life is not one of peace, but neither is it one of turmoil. You hold each experience up to the light of day and examine it for its essential truth. You think and rethink before coming to a conclusion about anything. An exquisite sensibility, beautifully crafted, is at work in each entry.

DORIS LESSING (1919–2013)

When you died, at the age of ninety-four, the media was filled with the news. You were, after all, a Nobel Prize winner whose work in a variety of genres through decade after decade continued to amaze. There are few books in the canon of women's writing that hold the stature of *The Golden Notebook*. Your personal life is an object lesson on the perils and rewards of risk taking. You were a part of all the great political movements of your time; sometimes at great personal cost.

Of all you have written, I feel most drawn to the little known *Alfred and Emily*. In that book, with the particular blend of creativity and generosity of spirit that infuses your life work, you reimagine the life of your parents. Here you were, eighty-eight years old, a legend in your own time, circling back to your beginnings; trying to imagine a better life for your parents.

And you were a truth teller up the very end:

> I amuse myself making definitions of old age: "When you wake up in the morning and are delighted that you don't have to go out that evening." "When every week you hear of some nasty disease some dear friend has succumbed to, and you have never even heard of it." "When you leaf through your address book and it is like strolling through a cemetery."

(2006)

TONI MORRISON (1931–)

It is the fiction for which you are best known. The African American experience and its lasting effects on every individual (black and white) touched by it have never been better portrayed. Those who come to you first through the movie depictions of your novels (as I did) may be surprised at the demands you make on the reader. The stories that connect so readily on a human level reach another dimension when rendered in your complex vocabulary and unique style.

You were a working, single mother for many years before recognition bought you the time needed to weave your commanding stories, your astute literary and societal criticism.

All your majesty is in the only quote from you that appears in this book—your speech upon receiving the Nobel Prize for Literature. The value of the old woman. The value of the word.

MAY SARTON (1912–1995)

Reading your journals in chronological order is like visiting an old mentor or friend yearly—noting her decline, rejoicing in signs of her "old self." And just when I have read one weather report or admired one floral arrangement too many comes a glimpse of your struggle to adapt to the challenges of failing health. It is strange to read of your symptoms—fatigue, declining strength, even constipation—years after your death. Yet there is strange comfort in picturing you preparing your bed for the night or deciding what to cook for supper—details that hardly anyone else would imagine worthy of publishing. As I perform these tasks myself, I remember you and the mindfulness you were able to bring to homely tasks. I also admire your active mind; the ease with which you quoted past readings from memory and your continued interest in the news of the day.

You never achieved the sort of literary recognition you craved. The poetry that you were perpetually working on was never revered; nor were the novels. Ironically, it was the journals of daily life that brought a steady stream of admiration and visitors your way.

FLORIDA SCOTT-MAXWELL (1883–1979)

One book—one indispensable record of an old woman's daily life—is all we have of you. Your history speaks of life as a playwright and as a Jungian therapist with few details. There is none of that in your book; or of the people who filled your early life or are around you in old age. There is one mention of a baby in your home, its intense concentration on the working of a small hole in its blanket. You do not say whose baby it is or anything else about the visit. In that detail is your essence: the close attention to the particular, the elevation of the individual to the universal.

You wrote that your seventies were relatively serene and so you were surprised with the jolt of renewed passion—for living, for appreciating, for wonderment—that arrived with your eighties. And you lived on to ninety-six! There is no one like you for chronicling the comforts of living alone, and the ways in which the powers of the mind can trump the encroaching deficits of the body.

EUDORA WELTY (1909–2001)

There are your wonderful novels, of course. They were written over time, with great care. But to me, the finest work you ever did was a short story done in a flash of outrage. Medgar Evers, a black civil rights leader, had been murdered by a white man in your town—Jackson, Mississippi. The story was published in the *New Yorker* less than a month later (July 1963). "Where is the Voice Coming From" had the murderer as narrator; his voice captured his fear, his ignorance, and the danger that abided in both. If you had been living in another part of the country, it would have been a literary act. Continuing to live as a white woman within the community, yours was an act of courage as well.

So I was not surprised to find the concluding words of your memoir, *One Writer's Beginnings*: "As you have seen, I am a writer who came of a sheltered life. A sheltered life can be a daring life as well. For all serious daring starts from within" (1983:144).

EDITH WHARTON (1862–1937)

Within the pages of your autobiography is the remarkable story of a woman who broke the bounds of expectations placed by an upper-class New York upbringing to become an internationally revered personage.

I picture you abed each morning, writing the pages that were to constitute your lasting legacy, and tossing them on the floor to be gathered and typed. Then you rose to face the day. You went everywhere. You knew everyone. You did war work in Paris. You created a magnificent home and garden in Lenox, Massachusetts, which continues to be visited by admirers of your taste and originality. Was there anything you could not do?

Your novels, never out of print, have been read, appreciated, made into films. Your travel and garden writing is less known but equally compelling. Your autobiography, unlike many others, speaks more about other people than yourself. Its first and last paragraphs, which I quote in these pages, offer me inspiration on the darkest days.

ANNOTATED READINGS

ACKERMAN, DIANE (1948–)

2012. *One Hundred Names for Love: A Memoir*. New York: Norton.

2009. *Dawn Light: Dancing with Cranes and Other Ways to Start the Day*. New York: Norton.

Ackerman is a naturalist who writes poetically in *Dawn Light* about her experience of the sunrise in the latitudes of her life and all that it evokes within her. *One Hundred Names for Love* is a moving story of a marriage under duress. When her husband suffers severe aphasia after a stroke, Ackerman devises a variety of ways to help him regain speech, preserve his independence, and continue the reciprocity that characterized their previous relationship.

ALLENDE, ISABEL (1942–)

2008. *The Sum of Our Days: A Memoir*. New York: HarperCollins.

Allende is known for fiction that takes place in politically tumultuous South American countries as well as a memoir of caring for a daughter who died after a long illness. This book describes Allende's day-to-day life as she faces the challenges and rewards of old age.

ANGELOU, MAYA (1928–2014)

2013. *Mom and Me and Mom*. New York: Random House.
2008. *Letter to My Daughter*. New York: Random House.
1997. *Even the Stars Look Lonesome*. New York: Random House.
1993. *Wouldn't Take Nothing for My Journey Now*. New York: Random House.
1981. *The Heart of a Woman*. New York: Random House.

> The memoir format is particularly suited to Angelou's style: short, punchy chapters that combine humor and wisdom. Angelou has lived a life encompassing many experiences, locales, relationships, and jobs, all of which appear on her pages. Recognizing characters and incidents from past volumes while seeing them anew through the author's maturing view is one of the special pleasures of reading the collection.

ATHILL, DIANA (1917–)

2008. *Somewhere Towards the End: A Memoir*. London: Granta.
2002. *Yesterday Morning*. London: Granta.

> Athill worked a lifetime as an editor of other people's work before retirement offered the opportunity to write in her own voice. In these two books Athill captures the origin and distills the essence of a worldview that offers comfort well into her nineties—and so offers a gift to the reader.

BATESON, MARY CATHERINE (1939–)

1990. *Composing a Life*. New York: Penguin Group.

> Bateson is the daughter of anthropologists Margaret Mead and Gregory Bateson. In this book, she uses an anthropological approach in discussing the life choices and directions of five women in late twentieth-century America. Equally adept at portraying the multiple societal forces and random life events that shape their lives and their individual styles, she paints a compelling portrait of mid- and late-life women after second-wave feminism.

BECHDEL, ALISON (1960–)

2012. *Are You My Mother?* New York: Houghton Mifflin Harcourt.
2006. *Fun Home: A Family Tragicomic.* Boston: Houghton Mifflin.

At the age of fifty-three, Bechdel is one of the younger authors quoted in this book. She is unique in that she is a graphic artist whose illustrations illuminate (and sometimes contradict) the verbal content of her life stories, providing a unique challenge and reward to the reader. Both memoirs discuss her life as a lesbian in the context of her early family experiences.

CASTLE, TERRY (1953–)

2010. "Travels with My Mother." In *The Professor and Other Writings*, 129–52. New York: HarperCollins.

Castle is that rare combination of academic and raconteur. In this book she shares personal experiences as well as interactions with such literary luminaries as Susan Sontag.

COLETTE (1873–1954)

1975. *Looking Backwards.* Bloomington: Indiana University Press.
1966. *Earthly Paradise: An Autobiography.* (Drawn from Colette's lifetime writings by Robert Phelps.) New York: Farrar, Straus & Giroux.
1963. *The Blue Lantern.* New York: Farrar, Straus & Giroux.
1961. *Break of Day.* New York: Farrar, Straus & Giroux.
1953. *My Mother's House and Sido.* New York: Farrar, Straus & Giroux. Introduction copyright 2001 by Judith Thurman.

Colette wrote gloriously and seemingly effortlessly about anything and everything that crossed her path throughout her adult life. Fiction borrowed themes from her life; nonfiction reads like poetry. Through wars and heartaches, illness and disability she wrote and wrote. The memoirs cited—a fraction of her input—were chosen because of their relevance to aging.

DE BEAUVOIR, SIMONE (1908–1986)

1973a. *The Coming of Age*. New York: Warner Paperbook Library Edition.
1973b. *A Very Easy Death*. New York: Warner Paperbook Library Edition.
1958. *Memoirs of a Dutiful Daughter*. New York: Harper & Row.
1949. *The Second Sex*. New York: Random House.

De Beauvoir and her life partner Sartre were legends in their own time: post–World War II Paris when existential theory was the rage. De Beauvoir's books on aging (*The Coming of Age*) and on women (*The Second Sex*)—combining a battery of statistical evidence buttressed by her analysis of social/cultural trends—were groundbreaking at the time of their publication. A half century later, some of the commentary remains trenchant while much content is dated and overintellectualized. Not so with the autobiography and story of the death of de Beauvoir's mother. Ironically titled, *Memoirs of a Dutiful Daughter* and *A Very Easy Death* show the vulnerable, human side of a noted intellectual of her time.

DIDION, JOAN (1934–)

2011. *Blue Nights*. New York: Knopf.
2005. *The Year of Magical Thinking*. New York: Knopf.
2003. *Where I Was From*. New York: Knopf.
1979. *The White Album*. New York: Simon and Schuster.
1961. *Slouching Toward Bethlehem: Essays*. New York: Farrar, Straus & Giroux.

Didion has tried her hand at fiction, but it is essays in which her true gifts emerge. These collections are filled with her insights and style.

DRABBLE, MARGARET (1939–)

2009. *The Pattern in the Carpet: A Personal History with Jigsaws*. New York: Houghton Mifflin Harcourt.

Drabble is known for her fictional depictions of the post–World War II educated classes in England. In this memoir she returns to her working-class roots and writes of a lifelong depression, its origin, and her efforts to transcend it.

DURAS, MARGUERITE (1914–1996)

1995. *C'est Tout*. New York: Seven Stories Press.
1987. *Practicalities*. New York: Grove Weidenfeld.

Duras, the revered author of *The Lover* and *Hiroshima, Mon Amour*, was a revered intellectual figure in Paris at the time of her death. Everything about her appeared outside of the mainstream: from her early years as a postcolonial émigré to France, through her adulthood as an increasingly desperate alcoholic and depressive. These memoirs—transcribed from her late life utterances—do not contradict her image so much as expand it.

ERNAUX, ANNIE (1940–)

2002. *The Possession*. New York: Seven Stories Press.
2000. *Happening*. New York: Seven Stories Press.
1999. *I Remain in Darkness*. New York: Seven Stories Press.
1992. *A Man's Place*. New York: Seven Stories Press.
1988. *A Woman's Story*. New York: Seven Stories Press.

Ernaux is a master of auto-fiction, stories from her own life in fictionalized form. In the writing cited here, she speaks of her obsession with a faithless lover (*The Possession*), an abortion at a time when it was illegal (*Happening*), re-creations of the lives of her parents (*A Man's Place* and *A Woman's Story*), and her mother's decline into dementia and death (*I Remain in Darkness*).

FISHER, M.F.K. (1908–1992)

1995. *Last House: Reflections, Dreams, and Observations, 1943–1991.* New York: Pantheon Books.

1993. *Stay Me, Oh Comfort Me: Journals and Stories, 1933–1941.* New York: Pantheon Books.

1992. *To Begin Again: Stories and Memoirs, 1908–1929.* New York: Pantheon Books.

1992. *The Ageless Spirit.* Edited by P. Berman and C. Goldman, 89–96. New York: Ballantine Books.

1984. *Sister Age.* New York: Random House.

1983. *Among Friends.* San Francisco: North Point Press.

1937. *The Art of Eating.* New York: Macmillan.

Fisher wrote incessantly throughout her long life; the cited writings are but a fraction of her output. All speak to a unique sensibility tethered to an extraordinary gift of expression.

FRENCH, MARILYN (1929–2009)

1998. *A Season in Hell: A Memoir.* New York: Knopf.

1977. *The Women's Room: A Novel.* New York: Ballantine Books.

French was a vocal proponent of second-wave feminism. *The Women's Room* is a fictional account of an academic's life at the height of the movement. *A Season in Hell* is a memoir of the last ten years of her life battling esophageal cancer. In it, she revisits her earlier days of social activism and reflects on the meaning of her life at its end.

GORDON, MARY (1949–)

2007. *Circling My Mother.* New York: Pantheon Books.

1996. *The Shadow Man: A Daughter's Search for Her Father.* New York: Random House.

Gordon is a noted writer of fiction who has written two memoirs about her parents. *Circling My Mother* is, as the title suggests, a collection of essays generated by the Alzheimer's disease and nursing home placement of her mother. *The Shadow Man* is about her own search for the truth behind the myths of an idealized father who died when she was young.

GORNICK, VIVIAN (1935–)

1988. *Fierce Attachments: A Memoir.* New York: Virago Press.

Gornick grew up in a working-class family in mid-twentieth-century New York. In this memoir the noted feminist and cultural critic writes of a life under the shadow of her father's early death, and the continuing nuances of her relationship with her mother.

GRUMBACH, DORIS (1918–)

2011. The view from 90. *American Scholar* (Spring).
2000. *The Pleasure of Their Company.* Boston: Beacon Press.
1996. *Life in a Day.* Boston: Beacon Press.
1994. *Fifty Days of Solitude.* Boston: Beacon Press.
1993. *Extra Innings: A Memoir.* New York: Norton.
1991. *Coming into the End Zone: A Memoir.* New York: Norton.

Grumbach is a cultural critic and novelist who began writing about her aging experience as she approached seventy. These memoirs plot her trajectory of experiences and changing attitudes.

HEILBRUN, CAROLYN G. (1926–2003)

1990. *Hamlet's Mother & Other Women.* New York: Columbia University Press.
1989. *Writing a Woman's Life.* New York: Ballantine Books.
1998. *The Last Gift of Time: Life Beyond Sixty.* New York: Random House.

Heilbrun was a distinguished professor and scholar of English literature as well as a writer of mysteries under the pen name of Amanda Cross. Her suicide at the age of seventy-seven produced shock waves through the many circles in which she was revered. *Hamlet's Mother* and *Writing a Woman's Life* are literary analyses of several texts seen through a feminist perspective. *The Last Gift of Time* contains a series of essays about life in her sixties.

JAMISON, KAY REDFIELD (1946–)

2009. *Nothing Was the Same: A Memoir.* New York: Knopf.

Jamison is a psychologist and medical school professor who has written extensively about her life experience with bipolar disorder. This memoir covers the year after the death of her husband.

L'ENGLE, MADELEINE (1918–2007)

1988. *Two-Part Invention: The Story of a Marriage.* San Francisco: HarperCollins.
1977. *The Irrational Season.* San Francisco: HarperCollins.
1974. *The Summer of the Great-Grandmother.* New York: Farrar, Straus & Giroux.

L'Engle is best known for *A Wrinkle in Time*, a science fiction fantasy with a fourteen-year-old female protagonist published in 1962 and in continuous print thereafter. Her deep understanding of science wedded to a deep religious faith is a hallmark of this author. The books cited are all journals written at her family's country house in Connecticut.

LERNER, GERDA (1920–2013)

1985. *A Death of One's Own.* Madison: University of Wisconsin Press.

Lerner was a noted academic who wrote one memoir—this depiction of her husband's life and death with cancer and all that she learned about caregiving and love through its process.

LESSING, DORIS (1919–2013)

2008. *Alfred and Emily.* New York: HarperCollins.

2006. Being 80: Old age is not for sissies. *AARP* (May/June).

2004. *Time Bites: Views and Reviews.* New York: Harper Perennial.

Lessing is renowned for the fiction and social activism that defined her adult life; chief among them *The Golden Notebook*, published in 1962. The works cited are late-life efforts. *Alfred and Emily* recreates the lives of her parents in post–World War I Rhodesia, the place of her birth. "Old Age Is Not for Sissies" and *Time Bites* are short essays.

MAIRS, NANCY (1943–)

1997. *Waist High in the World.* Boston: Beacon Press.

1993. *Ordinary Time: Cycles in Marriage, Faith, and Renewal.* Boston: Beacon Press.

Mairs was stricken with multiple sclerosis while still a young adult. The progression of the disease, coupled with her tendency toward depression and the cancer diagnosis of her husband, are the backdrop of these eloquent essays of life under duress.

MILLER, NANCY K. (1941–)

2002. *But Enough About Me: Why We Read Other People's Lives.* New York: Columbia University Press.

Miller is an academic and cultural critic who weaves her own life experiences into a literary dissection the genre of life writing.

MORRISON, TONI (1931–)

2002. *What Moves at the Margin: Selected Nonfiction.* Edited by Carolyn C. Denard. Jackson: University Press of Mississippi.

Morrison is known for her novels of African American life and the heritage of slavery (many of which were made into movies). Her speech upon acceptance of the 1993 Nobel Prize in Literature is included in this collection.

NIN, ANAÏS (1903–1977)

1980. *The Diary of Anaïs Nin*. Volume 7: *1966–1974*. New York: Harcourt Brace Jovanovich.

Nin is best known for the erotica and diaries she wrote during the 1930s in Paris. In volume 7, her last journal, she writes of her days living and dying with cancer.

OATES, JOYCE CAROL (1938–)

2011. *A Widow's Story: A Memoir*. New York: HarperCollins.

Oates is a prolific writer of fiction, essays, and literary criticism. *A Widow's Story* reflects the first year after the sudden death of her husband.

O'BRIEN, EDNA (1930–)

2013. *Country Girl: A Memoir*. Boston: Little, Brown.

O'Brien is best known for her fiction. *Country Girl* depicts her early years in Ireland and the effects of the experience on the rest of her life. She was, for many years, the toast of literary circles in London and New York, and this memoir contains interesting portrayals of famous people she met along the way.

OLIVER, MARY (1935–)

2004. *Essays and Other Life Writings*. Boston: Da Capo Press.
1999. *Winter Hours: Prose, Prose Poems, and Poems*. Boston: Houghton Mifflin.

Oliver is a prize-winning poet, best known for her depictions of the natural world. This collection provides a rare view into her private life and the sources of her inspiration.

PIERCY, MARGE (1936–)

2001. *Sleeping with Cats: A Memoir.* New York: William Morrow/HarperCollins.

Piercy is a poet, novelist, and social activist who grew up in working-class Detroit. *Sleeping with Cats* depicts her development as a writer and evolving contentment living by the sea with her partner and cats.

RICH, ADRIENNE (1929–2012)

2003. *What Is Found There: Notebooks on Poetry and Politics.* New York: Norton.

Rich is best known for her poetry and devotion to progressive political ideas. *What Is Found There* is a collection of her writings that offers rare insights into the origins of her personality and views.

ROIPHE, ANNE (1935–)

2008. *Epilogue: A Memoir.* New York: HarperCollins.
1999. *1185 Park Avenue: A Memoir.* New York: The Free Press.

Roiphe is known for her fiction, though *1185 Park Avenue* is a memoir of her childhood and coming of age. Its title is her first address. *Epilogue* is about the first year after her husband's death.

SARTON, MAY (1912–1995)

1996. *At Eighty-Two: A Journal.* New York: Norton.
1993. *Encore: A Journal of the Eightieth Year.* New York: Norton.

1992a. *The Ageless Spirit.* Edited by P. Berman and C. Goldman, 233–38. New York: Ballantine Books.

1992b. *Endgame: A Journal of the Seventy Ninth Year.* New York: Norton.

1988. *After the Stroke: A Journal.* New York: Norton.

1980. *Recovering: A Journal.* New York: Norton.

1977. *The House by the Sea: A Journal.* New York: Norton.

1976. *A World of Light: Portraits and Celebrations.* New York: Norton.

1973. *Journal of a Solitude: The Intimate Diary of a Year in the Life of a Creative Woman.* New York: Norton.

1968. *Plant Dreaming Deep.* New York: Norton.

May Sarton is a renowned for the journals of her middle to late life, listed here.

SCHWARTZ, LYNNE SHARON (1939–)

2009. *Not Now, Voyager.* Berkeley: Counterpoint,

Schwartz has written in many genres. *Not Now, Voyager* is a collection of her essays.

SCOTT-MAXWELL, FLORIDA (1883–1979)

1968. *The Measure of My Days.* New York: Penguin Books.

Scott-Maxwell is best known for this journal of life in her eighties.

SHULMAN, ALIX KATES (1932–)

2008. *To Love What Is: A Marriage Transformed.* New York: Farrar, Straus & Giroux.

1999. *A Good Enough Daughter.* New York: Schocken Books.

1995. *Drinking the Rain: A Memoir.* New York: Farrar, Straus & Giroux.

Shulman is equally prolific in fiction and nonfiction. These memoirs sequentially explore her relation to self (*Drinking the Rain*), to her parents (*A Good Enough Daughter*), and to her disabled husband (*To Love What Is*).

WALKER, ALICE (1944–)

2006. *We Are the Ones We Have Been Waiting For: Inner Light in a Time of Darkness*. New York: New Press.

Walker is most closely associated with *The Color Purple,* a Pulitzer Prize–winning novel about African American life. The work cited here consists of deep reflections on the circumstances of her life.

WELTY, EUDORA (1909–2001)

1983. *One Writer's Beginnings*. New York: Warner Books.
1963. "Where is the voice coming from?" *New Yorker* (July).

Welty's fiction of the southern experience and her insights into the racial divide that is the enduring legacy of slavery and segregation is much esteemed. In this autobiography, she traces the origin of her sensibility.

WHARTON, EDITH (1862–1937)

1933. *A Backward Glance: An Autobiography*. New York: Simon and Schuster.

Wharton wrote in many genres but is best known for her fiction of the upper classes of New York society at home and abroad in the early twentieth century. Her autobiography is filled with incidents of a fascinating life and wide acquaintance.

REFERENCES

Bloom, Amy. 2010. *Where the God of Love Hangs Out*. New York: Random House.

Burack-Weiss, Ann. 2006. *The Caregiver's Tale: Loss and Renewal in Memoirs of Family Life*. New York: Columbia University Press.

Butler, Robert N. 1963. The life review: An interpretation of reminiscence in the aged. *Psychiatry* 26:65.

Calasanti, Toni M., and Kathleen Slevin, eds. 2006. *Age Matters: Re-Aligning Feminist Thinking*. New York: Routledge.

Cole, Thomas R., W. Andrew Achenbaum, Patricia L. Jakobi, and Robert Kastenbaum, eds. *Voices and Visions of Aging: Toward a Critical Gerontology*. New York: Springer.

Conway, Jill Ker, ed. 1992. *Written by Herself: Autobiographies of American Women: An Anthology*. New York: Vintage Books, Random House.

Cruikshank, Margaret. 2009 [2003]. *Learning to Be Old: Gender, Culture, and Aging*. Lanham, Md.: Rowman and Littlefield.

Cummings, Elaine, and William Henry. 1961. *Growing Old*. New York: Basic Books.

Dulin, Agnes M. 2007. A lesson in social work role theory: An example of human behavior in the social environment. *Advances in Social Work* 8, 1.

Doka, Kenneth J. 2007. *Living with Grief: Before and After the Death*. Washington, D.C.: Hospice Foundation.

———. 1989. *Disenfranchised Grief*. Lexington, Mass: Lexington Press.

Friedan, Betty. 2013. *The Feminine Mystique*. 50th anniversary ed. New York: Norton.

———. 1993. *The Fountain of Age*. New York: Simon and Schuster.

Freud, Sigmund. 1917. *Mourning and Melancholia*. In *The Standard Edition of the Complete Psychological Works of Sigmund Freud*, vol. 14 (1914–1916). London: Hogarth Press.

Gilbert, Sandra. 2005. *Death's Door: Modern Dying and the Ways We Grieve*. New York: Norton.

Gornick, Vivian. 2001. *The Situation and the Story: The Art of Personal Narrative*. New York: Farrar, Straus & Giroux.

Halpern, Daniel, ed. 1990. *Our Private Lives: Journals, Notebooks and Diaries*. New York: Vintage Books.

Hearne, Betsy, and Roberta Seelinger Trites, eds. 2009. *A Narrative Compass: Stories That Guide Women's Lives*. Urbana. University of Illinois Press.

Kaufman, Sharon R. 1994. *The Ageless Self: Sources of Meaning in Late Life*. New York: New American Library.

Kenyon, Gary M., Jan-Eric Ruth, and Wilheml Mader. 1999. Elements of a narrative gerontology. In *Handbook of Theories of Aging*, 40–58. New York: Springer.

Konigsberg, Ruth D. 2011. *The Truth About Grief: The Myth of the Five Stages*. New York: Simon and Schuster.

Kübler-Ross, Elisabeth. 1969. *On Death and Dying: What the Dying Have to Teach Doctors, Nurses, Clergy, and Their Own Families*. New York: Scribner.

LeJeune, Philippe. 1989. *On Autobiography*. Minneapolis: University of Minnesota Press.

Myerhoff, Barbara. 2007. *Stories as Equipment for Living: Last Talks and Tales of Barbara Myerhoff*. Ann Arbor: University of Michigan Press.

Olney, James. 1998. *Memory and Narrative: The Weave of Life-Writing*. Chicago: University of Chicago Press.

Parini, Jay, ed. 1999. *The Norton Book of American Autobiography*. New York: Norton.

Ray, Ruth E. 2008. *Endnotes: An Intimate Look at the End of Life*. New York: Columbia University Press.

———. 2004. Toward the croning of feminist gerontology. *Journal of Aging Studies* 18:109–21.

Reynolds, Bertha Capen. 1942. *Learning and Teaching in the Practice of Social Work.* New York: Atheneum.

Riley, Matilda White, ed. 1972. A sociology of age stratification. In *Aging and Society*, vol. 3. New York: Russell Sage Foundation.

Rose, Phyllis, ed. 1993. *The Norton Book of Women's Lives.* New York: Norton.

Silverstone, Barbara, and Ann Burack-Weiss. 1983 *Social Work Practice with the Frail Elderly and Their Families: The Auxiliary Function Model.* Springfield, Ill.: Charles Thomas.

Wasser, Edna. 1966. *Creative Approaches in Casework with the Aging.* New York: Family Service Association of America.

———. 2003. Women aging. *Women's Review of Books* (July).